Cutting Plays for Performance

Cutting Plays for Performance offers a practical guide for cutting a wide variety of classical and modern plays. This essential text offers insight into the various reasons for cutting, methods to serve different purposes (time, audience, story), and suggests ways of communicating cuts to a production team.

Dealing with every aspect of the editing process, it covers structural issues, such as plot beats, rhetorical concepts, and legal considerations, why and when to cut, how to cut with a particular goal in mind such as time constraints, audience and storytelling, and ways of communicating cuts to a production team. A set of practical worksheets to assist with the planning and execution of cuts, as well as step-by-step examples of the process from beginning to end in particular plays help to round out the full range of skills and techniques that are required when approaching this key theatre-making task.

This is the first systematic guide for those who need to cut play texts. Directors, dramaturgs, and teachers at every level from students to seasoned professionals will find this an indispensable tool throughout their careers.

Toby Malone holds a PhD in Shakespearean textual analysis from the University of Toronto and is Assistant Professor of Dramaturgy at the State University of New York at Oswego. Select favorite cuts include *The Comedy of Errors* (Canadian Stage Company, Toronto), *Romeo + Juliet* (Driftwood Theatre, Toronto), *Hamlet (Variorum)* (Poorboy Theatre, Glasgow and Toronto), *A Midsummer Night's Dream* (Soulpepper, Toronto), *#R3* (University of Waterloo), and *King Lear* (Stratford Festival, Canada). He is a founding partner in subTEXT Dramaturgy Solutions and the Entertainment Engineering Collective and is an active member of the Literary Managers and Dramaturgs of the Americas and the Dramatists Guild of America.

Aili Huber holds an MFA in directing from Mary Baldwin University and the American Shakespeare Center. She has been directing for over 20 years. Favorite credits include *Sperm Donor Wanted* with Slow Your Role Theater Co., *Romeo and Juliet*, *The Duchess of Malfi*, *Antony and Cleopatra*, and *Richard III* with Pigeon Creek Shakespeare, *The Winter's Tale* at Bridgewater College, *Noye's Fludde* at Eastern Mennonite High School, and *JB* at Eastern Mennonite University. She is an associate member of the Stage Directors and Choreographers Society and the Shakespeare Theater Association, and a Tier 3 member of Directors Gathering.

"Anyone who stages Shakespeare's plays—and those of other leading playwrights—knows that to revive these works typically means to trim them. But how should they be cut? And at what cost? *Cutting Plays for Performance* brilliantly explores the techniques and approaches that govern how this is done. It's an original and practical book, one that actors, directors, scholars, and playgoers will find—as I have—an engrossing and invaluable read."

James Shapiro, Author of *1599: A Year in the Life of William Shakespeare*

"Drawing on interviews with some of the world's leading directors as well as their own experiences of the stage, Malone and Huber have produced a lively and engaging guide to an essential (but often invisible) component of any theatrical performance: cutting the text. With examples from across the dramatic canon and written in an accessible style, *Cutting Plays for Performance* is an indispensable resource for budding students, practitioners, and critics of theatre. I still can't believe this book hasn't existed until now."

Brett Greatley-Hirsch, Leeds University, UK

"In *Cutting Plays for Performance*, Aili Huber and Toby Malone offer practical and insightful tips suitable for the novice or an experienced practitioner. Their rich collection of insights and anecdotes from a variety of sources illuminates the travails and joys inherent in shaping text for performance. This resource will prove a valuable tool for teachers, directors, and dramaturgs."

Sarah Enloe, Shakespeare Theatre Association President

"*Cutting Plays for Performance* is pragmatic, firmly grounded in scholarship and theatre practice, and written with humour and clarity. One of the best ways of knowing what work is done by the individual components of a play, is to try taking them out, and this lively guide is a great place to start for anyone working with dramatic texts, whether as actor, director, dramaturg—or reader. Highly recommended!"

Russell Jackson, Emeritus Professor of Drama, University of Birmingham, UK and Script Advisor, Kenneth Branagh's Shakespeare films

Cutting Plays for Performance
A Practical and Accessible Guide

Toby Malone and Aili Huber

LONDON AND NEW YORK

Cover image: Cover art collage designed by Aili Huber. Permissions details can be found in the book's preliminary pages under "About the Cover Image".

First published 2022
by Routledge
4 Park Square, Milton Park, Abingdon, Oxon OX14 4RN

and by Routledge
605 Third Avenue, New York, NY 10158

Routledge is an imprint of the Taylor & Francis Group, an informa business

© 2022 Toby Malone and Aili Huber

The right of Toby Malone and Aili Huber to be identified as authors of this work has been asserted in accordance with sections 77 and 78 of the Copyright, Designs and Patents Act 1988.

All rights reserved. No part of this book may be reprinted or reproduced or utilised in any form or by any electronic, mechanical, or other means, now known or hereafter invented, including photocopying and recording, or in any information storage or retrieval system, without permission in writing from the publishers.

Trademark notice: Product or corporate names may be trademarks or registered trademarks, and are used only for identification and explanation without intent to infringe.

British Library Cataloguing-in-Publication Data
A catalogue record for this book is available from the British Library

Library of Congress Cataloging-in-Publication Data
A catalog record has been requested for this book

ISBN: 978-0-367-74892-0 (hbk)
ISBN: 978-0-367-74888-3 (pbk)
ISBN: 978-1-003-16007-6 (ebk)

DOI: 10.4324/9781003160076

Typeset in Bembo
by codeMantra

Toby Malone: To my dramaturgy mentor, the late, great Iris Turcott. Iris trusted me, an apprentice dramaturg, to offer my opinion on a cut when she had every right to expect I was just there to make coffee. What's more, she applied what I offered and kept asking what I thought. Iris encouraged me to take risks, ask questions, and to fearlessly challenge what was expected.

Aili Huber: To the Pigeon Creek Shakespeare Company where I got my start cutting plays. Your kindness, insight, and patience made learning the hard way easy.

Contents

List of Figures	ix
List of Interviews	xi
About the Cover Image	xiii
Acknowledgments	xv
Introduction	1
1 The Text is a Lie: Textual History and Why It Matters	10
2 Start Here: The Three Questions	22
3 The Cutter's Toolkit Part One: Materials	35
4 The Cutter's Toolkit Part Two: Strategies and Considerations	48
5 Cut to the Quick: Character-Specific Cuts	63
6 Don't Cut That! The Mechanics of Cuts	77
7 Cut to the Moment: Production-Specific Cuts	97
8 Scissors, Paste, and Negotiations: Communicating Cuts	118
Appendix 1: Legal Concerns	131
Appendix 2: Cut Activities	140
Appendix 3: Further Reading	143
Index	145

Figures

0.4	Image of toppling Jenga® Tower, open source, credit Shutterstock	6
1.3	Venn diagram of the *Dr. Faustus* A and B Texts, created by Aili Huber	14
1.5	Parallel-text spreadsheet of multiple texts of *King Lear*, created by Toby Malone	17
2.5	Freytag's Pyramid of Sophocles' *Oedipus Rex*, created by Toby Malone	31
3.2	Parallel-text spreadsheet of multiple texts of *Henry the Sixth, Part One*, created by Toby Malone	39
3.3	Image depicting the folding of Quarto and Folio pages, created by Toby Malone	41
3.5	Textual notes and excerpt from *Hamlet*, the Arden Shakespeare, ed. Edward Dowden, 1899. Reproduced under fair use	43
3.6	Textual notes and excerpt from *Hamlet*, the Internet Shakespeare Editions (ed. David Bevington) and the Folger Shakespeare (ed. Barbara A. Mowat and Paul Werstine). Reproduced under fair use	44
4.3	Image from *Machinal*, featuring Alex Hedly, Vincent Boyer, Brendan Christ, Emily Dempsey, John Le, Thomas Perry, Kelleigh Stevenson, Seun Sule. Directed by Maria Soyla Enriquez. Set and lighting design by Matthew Mitra. Costume design by Maria Soyla Enriquez. Photo by Sharon Siegfried, courtesy of Penn State Harrisburg	53
4.6	Word cloud diagrams of the *Dr. Faustus* A- and B-Texst, created by Aili Huber	60
4.7	Parallel-text spreadsheet comparing Shakespeare's F1 *Romeo and Juliet* with Julian Fellowes' 2013 adaptation, created by Toby Malone	61
6.1	Unstressed syllables move slowly when they come as single spies, but rush along in battalions	78
6.2	Rhetorical analysis of *Romeo and Juliet*, created by Cass Morris	87

7.3	Summer camp student actors take a bow at the end of *Much Ado About Nothing* at the American Shakespeare Center, directed by Aili Huber, 2016. Photo by Lindsey Walters	103
7.4	Image depicting inside the newly renovated auditorium of the Stratford Festival's Tom Patterson Theatre. Photography by doublespace photography	105
7.5	Image from the world premiere of *Hecate*, adapted and directed by Kylie Bracknell [Kaarljilba Kaardn], and translated by Kylie Bracknell [Kaarljilba Kaardn] & Dr Clint Bracknell. Presented by Yirra Yaakin Theatre Company in association with Bell Shakespeare. A Perth Festival commission. Photograph by Dana Weeks	107
7.6	Image from *R3 (Richard III)*, Written by William Shakespeare, Adapted by Toby Malone, Directed by Jennifer Roberts-Smith, Set design by William Chesney, Costume design by Sharon E. Secord, Lighting design by Hilary Pitman, Video design by Tallen Kay, Pictured from left to right: (background) – Jessica Blondin (Catesby), Erik Johnson (Brakenbury); (foreground) – Kandi Prosser (Lady Anne Neville), Leah Magdalen (Queen Elizabeth), Meghan Jones (The Duchess of York). Photo courtesy of the University of Waterloo	112
7.7	Kate Mulvany as Richard III in Bell Shakespeare's 2017 production *Richard 3*, directed by Peter Evans. Photo by Prudence Upton	113
7.8	Image from Pigeon Creek Shakespeare's *Richard III*, Grand Haven, Michigan. Directed by Aili Huber. Costume design by Kate Bode. Featuring Kate Bode (Queen Margaret) and Katherine Mayberry (Queen Elizabeth). Photograph by Seraphina Zorn	115
8.4	Digital tools screenshot of a cut of *Antony and Cleopatra*, created by Aili Huber	123
8.5	Prompt book facsimile from David Garrick's *A Midsummer Night's Dream* (Drury Lane, London, 23 November 1734), PROMPT M.N.D 06. Folger Shakespeare Library Call #: 54843. Used by permission of the Folger Shakespeare Library	124
8.7	Image of James Evans and Kyle Morrison in rehearsal for Bell Shakespeare's 2021 Australian national tour of *A Midsummer Night's Dream*. Courtesy of Bell Shakespeare, photo by Brett Boardman	126
A1.2	Image of the Dramatists Guild of America Bill of Rights. Artwork Design by Bekka Lindstrom used with permission from The Dramatists Guild of America, the national trade association playwrights, composers, lyricists, and librettists	134

Interviews

Anne Bogart, Artistic Director, SITI Company, New York City. 8 March 2021.
Tim Carroll, Artistic Director, Shaw Festival, Niagara-on-the-Lake, Ontario. 28 January 2021.
Antoni Cimolino, Artistic Director, Stratford Festival, Canada, Stratford, Ontario. 12 February 2021.
Amy R. Cohen, Catherine Ehrman Thoresen '23 and William E. Thoresen Professor of Speech and Theatre, Chair of the Theatre Department, Professor of Classics, Randolph College, Lynchburg, Virginia.
Ralph Alan Cohen, Founding Executive Director and Senior Advisor at the American Shakespeare Center, Staunton, Virginia. 24 November 2020.
Lue Morgan Douthit, Executive Director of Play On Shakespeare, Oregon. 24 February 2021.
James Evans, Associate Director, Bell Shakespeare, Sydney. 1 February 2021.
Linda Hutcheon, Professor Emeritus, University of Toronto, author, *A Theory of Adaptation*. 25 May 2021.
Martine Kei Green-Rogers, Professor at SUNY New Paltz, freelance dramaturg and past president of the Literary Managers and Dramaturgs of the Americas. 28 January 2021.
Megan McDonough, Cultural Programs Coordinator at Conejo Recreation and Parks District, California. 9 February 2021.
Grant Mudge, Ryan Producing Artistic Director, Notre Dame Shakespeare, Indiana. 22 January 2021.
Kate Mulvany, actor, text editor, playwright, and dramaturg, Sydney/New York City. 14 February 2021.
Anna Northam, freelance actor, UK. 1 March, 2021
Peter Oswald, freelance playwright and translator, London. 11 February 2021.
Tina Packer, Founding Artistic Director, Shakespeare & Company, Lenox, Massachusetts. 10 March 2021.
Christine Schmidle, Deputy Text Associate at Shakespeare's Globe, London, director of Vision and Text at Flagstaff Shakespeare Festival. 4 December 2020.

James Shapiro, professor and author (*1599, Contested Will*), text editor for The Public Shakespeare, New York City. 8 February 2021.

Caridad Svich, OBIE-award winning playwright, New York City. 5 February 2021

TJ Young, playwright and dramaturg, Pittsburgh, PA. 9 February 2021

About the Cover Image

Aili Huber designed this collage. The images included, from top left to bottom right, are: The Blackfriars Playhouse at the American Shakespeare Center, photo by Lindsey Walters; the script of *Give Us Good*, by Pam Mandigo, edited during rehearsal by toddler dramaturg Silas Anansi Huber; a parallel text comparison of the A-Text and B-Text of *Dr. Faustus*, prepared by Toby Malone for *Blast Faustus*, part of Poorboy Theatre Scotland's *Blast Classics* series, 2012; Katherine Mayberry and Scott Lange as Cleopatra and Antony. Photo by Chaz Albright, costume design by Roz Srb. Pigeon Creek Shakespeare Company, 2019; Jessica Blondin (Catesby), Kandi Prosser (Lady Anne Neville), Leah Magdalen (Queen Elizabeth Woodville), in *#R3 (Richard III)*, University of Waterloo, 2013; a page of Aristophanes' *The Frogs*; prompt book from David Garrick's *A Midsummer Night's Dream* (Drury Lane, London, 23 November 1734), PROMPT M.N.D 06. Folger Shakespeare Library Call #: 54843. Used by permission of the Folger Shakespeare Library; 18th-Century engraved print of Susanna Centlivre; the "Chandos portrait" of William Shakespeare, possibly by John Taylor; rhetorical analysis of *Romeo and Juliet* by Cass Morris; Aili Huber's cut of *Antony and Cleopatra* using digital tools; Toby Malone's cut of *Richard III* using manual tools; James Shapiro's cut of *Coriolanus*; a page from *Thomas More*, possibly in Shakespeare's hand; *Ira Aldridge in the Role of Shakespeare's Othello* by William Mulready; word cloud of *Miss Julie*; compilation script of *Queen Margaret*, edited by Megan McDonough.

Acknowledgments

Thanks to …

Kennedy Center American College Theater Festival Region 2, the American Shakespeare Center, the Stratford Festival, Canada, Kate Bode, Sujata Iyengar, Kat Hermes, Scott Lange, Jemma Levy, Sally-Beth MacLean, Katherine Mayberry, Meg Miroshnik, Ann Pleiss Morris, Cass Morris, David Ryding, Sandy Thomson, Janelle Rainville, Barret Ogden, Jennifer Roberts-Smith, Ann Swerdfager, Russell Jackson, Patrick W. Mathis, Brett Greatley-Hirsch, Eric Johnson, Melanie Leung, Tamar Thomas, Emmanuel Wilson, and Kenneth Branagh.

Special thanks to our families—JC, Silas, and Petra Huber and Meg, Cormac, and Bridie Malone—for graciously sparing us the time and space we needed to write this book.

The concept for this book began as a workshop Aili and Toby taught at the 51st annual Kennedy Center American College Theater Festival, Region 2, in Montclair, NJ, on 18 January 2019. The workshop was entitled "The First Thing We Do, Let's Cut All the Lawyers: How to Cut Shakespeare." This joke (a reference to a line from Shakespeare's *Henry the Sixth Part Three*) made it as far as the original book proposal, as "The First Thing We Do," a pun with real meaning for a cut's place in the production process. Logic prevailed in consultation with our editors as we set our final title.

An earlier version of Chapter 7's "Virtual Logistics" segment appeared in an article entitled "Cutting and Adapting Text for the Virtual Performing Landscape" in *New & Noteworthy: The LMDA Newsletter*, Vol. 6, No. 4 (December 2020).

Introduction

Hamlet. Act Two, Scene Two. A group of travelling players have arrived at Elsinore. Our inspired title character exhorts his guests to reprise one of their past performances: an epic depiction of the fall of Troy. One player steps up with relish and performs the evocative scene with details, images, and free-flowing descriptors. Sixty lines into the speech, Hamlet remains enthralled. Not everyone shares his enthusiasm: Polonius, the pedantic politician, has become impatient.

"This is too long."

The nerve! Hamlet is exasperated. Too long? What are they supposed to do? Cut it?

Not necessarily. But believe it or not, yes, a cut might be the best solution of all. To many directors, dramaturgs, and actors, cutting plays is an integral step in the process of theatre. Cuts might happen in deep pre-production, or at a table read, or in rehearsal, or even, quite rarely, in performance. Cuts happen to control the play's length, to address modesty issues or cultural differences, or to fit a directorial concept. Cuts are common. Standard, even.

To an outsider, cuts may seem audacious, hubristic, or even sacrilegious. *You want to cut a play a playwright has authorized as complete? Who do you think you are?* Such dismay has historical precedent. The famously opinionated George Bernard Shaw believed if you can't perform Shakespeare uncut, then you shouldn't perform it at all. The plays, Shaw suggested, were that length and had that content for a purpose. To change the content was to remove some of the play's spirit: in his inimitable style, Shaw suggested adapters "let Shakespear alone if you dont believe in him" (sic, Stone-Blackburn, 46). Without a doubt, Shaw would be horrified to know how often his own works are cut to size today.

To the purists, cuts may seem like unnecessary brutality inflicted on a beloved text, perpetrated out of fear of a classical play's inherent intricacy. In fact, cutting is not only common but also necessary. Polonius's instinctive, "This is too long," does not necessarily betray a lack of sophistication, but perhaps an audience's very real awareness they are no longer engaged. A company may faithfully retain every line in an original practice staging of Aeschylus's *The Persians* (472 BCE), yet might potentially undermine their

DOI: 10.4324/9781003160076-1

Kate Mulvany:
I was raised with this idea that "you can't cut Shakespeare. He's the king. You can't chop off the finger of the king."

0.1 Excerpt from interview with Kate Mulvany, 14 February 2021.

narrative if the audience's attention wanders. Another company may insist their production of Aphra Behn's *The Rover* (1677) is letter-perfect and have the time and audience to embrace it. When these rare opportunities for uncut performance arrive, they can be instructive and fulfilling, albeit quite long.

So, the question is, what do you cut? And how? And what happens to the rest of the play? Is it the same play? What about the purists? *Is* this sacrilegious?

Context

Everyone has opinions about what is acceptable to cut and what is indispensable. The line between practicality and blasphemy is intensely personal. Both authors have experienced pushback on countless occasions, from collaborators whose demarcation differed. In one instance, a fellow director scolded Aili for cutting the messenger at the beginning of *Much Ado About Nothing* (1598): without this messenger to match the one at the end, he insisted, the play was out of balance. In another setting, Toby opted to trim so much from a single character, the actor finally, peevishly, said, at the outset of their next line, "Am I *allowed* to say this? Or are you gonna cut it too?" Cuts can cut deep.

This very book began as an argument over what one can acceptably cut. Faced with the daunting task of producing a high-school-appropriate, 100-minute cut of Shakespeare's *Richard III* (1593, the second-longest play in the canon, just after *Hamlet*), Aili shared a thought experiment with Toby. "I'm thinking of cutting out everything that happens at Pomfret. It's confusing because my audience won't even know who Rivers and Grey are!" Toby, a scholar with deep roots in this play's performance history, countered, noting one couldn't simply lop out those entire scenes and characters: what about the familial texture it offers? This led to a spirited, enjoyable debate; we challenged our assumptions about "acceptable" cuts, and cuts which go "too far," clarified our own reasons, and discovered a trove of questions we couldn't quite answer. This debate turned into a longer conversation on process and style. We shared many similar tools in our approach, yet we also deviated wildly. Fast forward to our completion of this volume. After conversations on cutting with 19 artists and luminaries from around the world, two things were eminently clear: not one of them was *taught* to cut in a classroom or a formal setting, and everyone does it in their own particular way, which is usually the result of being "thrown in the deep end."

James Shapiro:
It's kind of like doing surgery: don't try this at home. Anybody can probably think they can do more than take out a splinter, but reconstructive surgery requires skill and training.

0.2 Excerpt from interview with James Shapiro, 8 February 2021.

To suggest that a successful cut emerges from "the deep end" might be cold comfort for the neophyte text editor. The deeper into the process a textual editor gets, the more questions tend to flow. A play is made up of dozens of moving parts. Play adapters, directors, and dramaturgs carefully balance considerations of length, clarity, narrative, character, design, logistics, and feasibility long before an audience sees the play. The audience, of course, represents the prime litmus test for the entire production. If your production of *The Little Clay Cart* (5th century CE) is six hours long and you fear for your audience's patience, some minor line cuts might be a means of expedience. If your production of *Man and Superman* (1903) is bogged down in Shavian details, a cut might clear the way: but, as we'll discuss, you may lose some incredible texture.

Although rarely acknowledged publicly, cutting is almost universal. Just about every company that stages classical theatre cuts every production, every playwright, every character, in some way, from tweaks to slashes. Rarely is anyone taught *how*. Cutting is traditionally positioned as a skill to "feel" your way through. To operate on blind faith and instinct has its merits—both of us learned to cut in the crucible of pre-production. We have developed a sense of cut pitfalls, and on some points reached different conclusions. We want to save others from the pain and embarrassment of taking a deeply flawed cut to a production team—or worse, an audience—and highlight aspects of the process where reasonable people might disagree.

Both authors have stood where, perhaps, you stand now. Faced with a monolithic classic which seems unquestionable and iconic, the process of undertaking a cut can be daunting and stressful. A poorly thought-out cut can undermine a play's structure and remove elements foundational to how the audience understands it. A thoughtless character removal or scene re-arrangement that seems logical in pre-production can be a detrimental rehearsal-time-waster.

This book, then, is a practical and accessible guide for how to go about those cuts, be you an overwhelmed beginner or a tip-curious veteran.

At first blush, and to the dispassionate outsider (an audience member, a producer, your mother) cuts may be an afterthought, or even a non-factor. The uninitiated—anyone who's never had to take on the task—might

> **Lue Douthit:**
> You have to think of this as like baking. I'm not a good baker, but I'll say that when you have to reduce the recipe, it's not just by half. There's a little too much baking soda or powder if you do it that way. Do you know what I mean? There's something you still have to figure out what that organic thing is. And of course, your context: ten actors, high school, going around to you know, multi purpose rooms, is perfectly valid. And in the assignment, right, versus like the 120 performances on the main stage of the Oregon Shakespeare Festival. What's that thing? The behemoth thing, right? So you have to look at it that way too, with all the context.

0.3 Excerpt from interview with Lue Douthit, 24 February 2021.

ask: "How hard can it be, honestly? Why not just cut lines as you go in rehearsal? If it doesn't work, add them back in. Take out boring stuff. Or hard stuff. Unfunny lines can just be cut out, along with redundant characters. The play's running long? What if we just remove Act III?"

All of this, of course, is hyperbolic, particularly the latter suggestion: to cut Act III of *any* play is to fundamentally and foundationally impact the piece. The playwright has written a play to communicate a story. That story is usually multi-layered: Ibsen's *Ghosts* (1881) isn't just about Oswald's syphilis, but also presses on the nature of Engstrand's goodness, class difference, and the fatality of life. A director may choose to focus on one or another of those strands to emphasize a theme, but to entirely cut one? There's the point at which the play starts to suffer.

To illustrate: Hamlet describes what he reads as mere "words, words, words," but is it so simple? As a unified statement, "Words, words, words," holds intrinsic meaning. Hamlet can express his frustration, his boredom, his carefree nature, his supposed madness through these three words. But what if, for some bizarre justification of time, an editor cuts one of those "words"? Or two?

POLONIUS: What is't that you read, my lord?
HAMLET: Words. Words.

POLONIUS: What is't that you read, my lord?
HAMLET: Words.

To trim only one or two "words" has a distinct impact on Hamlet's line: the rule of three cements his tone. It allows the actor to use the repetition as emphasis or to speak each of the "words" in a different, pointed manner. To remove one or two of those "words" will also alter the flow of the line and will likely hit the ear of any educated listener as absent. They are tiny, imperceptible cuts, but they are also enormous, audience-rattling cuts; to not consider the impact of changes is risky. Worse, haphazardly removing those words can destabilize the text.

It can be like an artlessly played game of Jenga®.

Bear with us here for a moment. Jenga®, as we're sure you know, is a popular family parlor game created in the 1970s by Leslie Scott and currently marketed by Hasbro. This deceptively simple game involves a package of 54 small rectangular wooden blocks, set up as a tower. The tower is built with layers of three blocks arranged on top of each other. Players must remove a block from somewhere in the tower, and make sure the entire structure does not topple. Take out the wrong piece, or do so without care, and *game over*.

Cutting can often look like a game of Jenga®. Early on, it seems simple: cut a speech here, remove a theme there, splice two characters over here. But there are few better ways to witness the playwright's art than to try to unravel it. Playwrights include themes, scenes, characters, and phrases for a purpose, and often a cut reminds you, scenes later, how the lines you removed actually provide useful context. Cut too much without thought on the play's narrative tendrils, and you run into new problems. Your Jenga® tower starts to wobble as you lose structural integrity.

Your combination of Rosencrantz and Guildenstern into an unholy hybrid called "Rosenstern" might make you laugh and save you a casting choice, but the lost texture means those characters' more urgent late-play moments become not only more complex, but stand out as false, and, worse, might elicit a chuckle from the audience at the wrong moment. To pare away the villagers' tales of the murder of the Polish merchant in Leopold Lewis' *The Bells* (1871) might save you 15 minutes but undermines the later graphically dramatic reveal that shows Matthias's memory of the crime. Lines and elements are there for a reason. Even so, many of those plays are long. Or complicated. Or feature elements that cannot be easily explained away in the modern world. So, we cut them—even if it's as simple as what Antoni Cimolino described to us as "a haircut"—without the Jenga® tower's demise.

Methodology

Both authors have experienced this process in multiple guises. As a director. As a dramaturg. As an actor. As a stage manager. We want to lay out a plan to make it clear how cuts have consequences. They must be justified. We should be aware of what we lose—and, perhaps, gain.

Throughout this book, we guide you through strategies for text cuts, based on our practical experience and conversations with other industry professionals. We will unpack the historical context of cutting to arm you against any critics who believe, Shaw-like, it is heresy.

You might observe how parts of this book seem dedicated to arguments for *not* cutting particular elements. "This line is vital," we might say. "Without it,

0.4 Don't let your cut bring your whole production crashing down.

the audience will be confused about where the letter came from." Or, "Without this character, who will go get the prince to bring him to the coronation?" We have even joked we should call the book *Don't Cut That!*, a quip that survives in the heading for our mechanics chapter. This is part of the purpose of why this book exists: a way to articulate and identify the many reasons *not* to cut elements—essentially, to get to *really* know your play—to ultimately clear the way to cut freely. We must dig into *why* various elements are present in the plays. Or, as our colleague Jemma Levy noted: "You never cut anything you don't understand. If you want to cut it, you have to *get* it first." You shouldn't cut something without having a good guess about why the playwright put it in there to begin with. What function does it serve in the story? Can you tell your story without it? If you don't know why it's there, you can't plan around its absence. Internationally lauded director Tim Carroll sometimes cuts at least 50% of the play as he prepares, purely as an exercise to see what parts are most important to him. In a similar vein, this book will help identify why specific elements are present in the text and, in turn, offer strategies to accommodate their removal, or advocate for their preservation.

Finally, we also take into account the immovable reality that for many plays, cutting is not a matter of *heresy*: it is a matter of *copyright*. Plays written in the last 75 or 80 years, dependent on your location, are protected by authors' copyright. *This means they cannot be cut.* Every case study in this book covers plays which are in the public domain in the United States, and either are in, or will soon enter, the public domain elsewhere.

This book is designed for processes of cutting plays legally permissible to cut. If you're not sure, please check with the rights holder of the work, listed on its copyright page.

While we expect some of the plays we feature to be quite familiar to you, we are thrilled to include lesser-known texts. Our attempts to select from a diverse range of playwrights were somewhat thwarted by copyright law; the playwrights of the Harlem Renaissance are only just coming into the public domain. We hope these examples spark your curiosity and prompt you to read *The Black Doctor* (1847) or *A Bold Stroke for a Husband* (1783). Don't feel like you're out of your depth if you don't know all these texts; in every case, we are careful to provide sufficient context on the play to follow the point we exemplify, even if you don't know the show.

What to expect

As you read through this guidebook, remember this is designed to offer action-tested perspectives on cuts. We place cut texts on their feet to see where they fall apart and find approaches we might not have considered based exclusively on theory. We lay out strategies, ideas, and considerations to form a core to any cut process, built on an assumption your play is available to be cut. Much of what we discuss emerges from personal experience: cavalier cuts which force a hurried regroup, or meek cuts which result in an anemic, disjointed script. We have cut for the purposes of time, physical space, audience, cast size, and director's concept. We have experienced cuts to foreground a central theme or experimental ideology, and to add clarity or sense.

As a collaborative work, we have found instances where our techniques diverge significantly, and points where we disagree on both process and outcome. We see the benefits in these differences. They emphasize there is no single "correct way" to cut theatrical texts. There are different approaches and strategies, all of which hopefully lead to the same goal—a successful performance. As Tina Packer said, on the various practices at Shakespeare & Company: "We don't have any prescription about how you should cut the plays. I think it's kind of important not to." If you have cut scripts yourself and find yourself disagreeing with our opinions, just remember: we offer strategies which have worked for us and may well work for you. But they're not the be-all and end-all. Each step we outline is flexible, as every production is different. If you attempt two separate cuts of *The Prince of Homburg* (1821) with two separate directors (although if you find yourself with two separate versions of *The Prince of Homburg* in quick succession, then congratulations, you live in an extremely literate community), you may find what worked for one doesn't fit with the other. So approach this book with that in mind: we offer perspectives and advice, but will never position this as *the* way. It's *a* way.

This volume features frequent call-outs where we converse on process with a collection of highly respected directors, dramaturgs, artistic directors, playwrights, actors, and editors from across the English-speaking world. Cutting dramatic texts is one of those shadowy behind-the-scenes acts, and each interviewee was eager to discuss their process. They rarely have an opportunity to talk about it. We bring these varied perspectives into the light not only to demonstrate cutting's efficacy, but to make the process accessible enough to be of use to educators and artists alike.

In one of these interviews, Anne Bogart reminded us to listen to our inner wisdom as we approach these texts:

> Study, study, study, and study the text again, and after that, study some more. But when the time comes, make the cuts quickly and intuitively, not logically. The logic is in you, so that the necessary leap-taking and intuition can kick in at that decisive moment. Otherwise, the cutting is academic. Lean on the poetry that is available to one's intuition.

We offer tools to support your logic, but you should not disregard your gut. We hope this will give your imagination new avenues, but not rigid rules.

We would like to encourage you to be open to surprises. You may be entirely convinced you have the right answer, only to be surprised by someone—maybe an actor, or a dramaturg, or a sound designer—who shows you another way to read the text, another way to understand what is necessary. While some of our advice may feel obvious to you, we hope that the insights we have gathered from industry luminaries will spark new paradigms on cutting. As we complete this book, Aili is in the process of preparing a production of *Measure for Measure*. Inspired by conversations with Martine Kei Green-Rogers and Tim Carroll, she's working on a radical experiment with sequencing time. Without this project, she wouldn't have considered that. We hope similar discoveries will arise for you.

Our *Richard III* argument has a useful coda. Aili produced two cuts of the play with the same company; the student matinee cut did indeed axe Pomfret. But another aspect of the cut surprised Toby. Aili's version favored the women. She rejected the common choice to conflate Margaret and the Duchess of York, which allowed the full force of their individual grief to propel the play forward. Men, especially Richard, had large cuts in their lines. The women's voices filled the space. Toby, on seeing this cut, wrote,

"It's amazing when you spend years of your adult life immersed in a play, and then you're knocked sideways with an exactly on-point reading that opens up so many doors." Sometimes, the power of a cut is not in what it removes, but what it reveals.

Happy trimming.

Works cited

Stone-Blackburn, Susan. "Shaw on Cutting Shakespeare." *The Shaw Review* 22:1 (January 1979), pp. 46–49.

1 The Text is a Lie
Textual History and Why It Matters

When we first tell people outside of the classical theatre bubble we're writing a book on play cuts, they are often mildly scandalized. "Are you *allowed* to *cut* a play?" they ask. "Won't people be upset if they don't see the whole thing?" Most spectators are unaware that nearly all productions of classical plays are cut or adapted. Our shocked interlocutors have likely never seen a complete production of any classical play. We would argue, for many play texts, no such thing currently exists—or, in many cases, ever did.

Let's look at the history of how the texts from as far back as ancient Greece have come down to us and how performers through time have edited them to suit their circumstances.

We begin with playtexts in an abstract sense. Imagine a theatre company, anywhere in the world, prior to easy and inexpensive print technology. This is the era of hand-copied text, or maybe meticulously typeset blocks for the printing press. This company is located in a capital city, where it can expect high-ranking government officials to be both financial patrons and audience members. A king or emperor may invite them to perform at court. In seasons when the wealthy leave the city, the company may go on the road and tour to remote regions. They have a few actors who always get the big roles, a few journeymen learning the craft, and occasional ringers when they need someone to carry a spear and say a line or two. They work with a few playwrights regularly. The playwrights grow so familiar with the actors they sometimes write parts just for them. To readers who know the history of Shakespeare's company, this may sound familiar. It will also ring a bell for readers who have studied the theatre of the medieval Mongol Yuan dynasty. The conditions by which professionals created plays before the invention of the typewriter followed a convergent evolution, where similar circumstances, separated by oceans and centuries, yielded similar adaptations.

In this theatre, the playwright creates a version of the play which communicates what needs to happen. This version, however, may not constitute what we think of as a completed text. The specific words of a speech might all be present, but so will notes to the actors like, "At this point, he explains the plot," without the exact explanation written out. Scribes copy out the play—at least one complete copy to be sent to the government censors

DOI: 10.4324/9781003160076-2

James Shapiro:
I no longer think anyone can stand a three-hour Shakespeare production. I'm increasingly a believer in two-hour Shakespeare: one thing I say when I come into a room is "I know the lengths of all these plays, from a four-hour *Hamlet* down to *Macbeth* or *The Comedy of Errors* at the other end." Shakespeare wrote plays—and I'm stealing from David Kastan, the Yale Professor here—Shakespeare wrote texts that were too long to be staged. He knew when he wrote *Hamlet* that it could not be staged in the spring or fall when daylight ended around 5:00pm and the plays began around 2:00pm, so Burbage would have been killed in a swordfight in the dark had it been run in full length. So he wrote "maximal texts" because he knew he had to pay the Master of the Revels to approve a text. You could cut but you couldn't add, so you write long. And the argument I make is Shakespeare's always been cut going back to original productions. So the argument that there's this imaginary purist who's trying to protect the text from cutting would have run into a buzzsaw of opposition from Burbage and the other Chamberlain's Men 400 years ago. That's just a fantasy.

1.1 Excerpt from interview with James Shapiro, 8 February 2021.

(a factor in nearly all art, for nearly all of recorded history) for review, and possibly another for the theatre management to hold.

Each actor would receive only their own part, plus a few cue lines here and there. Very few copies of the complete play document exist at this point. As changes happen, either in rehearsal or in response to government intervention, some play documents have notes scribbled in their margins and lines marked out, but not every emendation makes it into every copy. Once the play is in performance, if it does well, documents begin to circulate publicly, sometimes in unauthorized forms hastily collated by unscrupulous text pirates. For some plays, several variants might circulate at the same time. To avoid financial losses in book sales, the theatre company might be forced to release updated "authorized editions," which now have the stubbed-in bits completed. Either the playwright or some functionary of the theatre company replaces "He explains the plot," with content to detail the explanation.

Meanwhile, the company receives an invitation to perform the play at court. They decide they'll remove the politically sensitive allusions the censor somehow missed. They don't want to upset their royal patron and land in jail. A few months later, disease shuts down the theatres, and the company packs their costumes and props into wagons and takes to the road. Within a couple of performances, they decide to axe the topical jokes about court gossip which padded a costume change in the third act and replace it with physical humor. They cross a border and find themselves among people with whom they don't share a language, so they cut out long speeches and use more visual storytelling. A couple years later, they revive the play. If they are fairly certain it will be a hit, they take the financial risk of adding references to current events, swallowing the cost of paying the playwright and additional review by government censors. They liberally cut bits out of sync with current fashion. Now we have many versions of the play, any or all of which may exist as printed documents: a bootleg of the first performance, an "official" version as performed before their majesties, a marked-up prompt book from the tour, and the version of the later revival the censor held. Which, then, is the "complete" version of the play?

Peter Oswald:
It's nice that there's instability: it leaves some leeway for interpretation.

1.2 Excerpt from interview with Peter Oswald, 11 February 2021.

We will now take a specific deeper dive into Shakespeare, simply because we assume our readers are generally more familiar with *Hamlet* (1601) than with *The Orphan of the House of Zhao* (c.13th century). The transmission of Shakespeare's texts is also a thoroughly examined and documented field of study. However, please understand we use Shakespeare purely as an example. Due to the volatile print culture of the Elizabethan and Jacobean ages, every idea we illustrate with the textual history of Shakespeare's plays is true of his contemporaries across Europe and has close parallels in other times and places. For example, Marlowe's *Dr. Faustus* was published in two distinct editions, in 1604 (today colloquially known as the 'A-Text') and 1616 (the 'B-Text'). Marlowe himself died in 1593, so the earliest published edition of this play post-dates him by more than a decade, while the 1616 version featured revisions more than 20 years after his grisly end. While the question of the A- and B-Texts of *Dr. Faustus* has yielded generations of spirited debate (see, in particular, Eric Rasmussen's *A Textual Companion to 'Dr Faustus'*), it is clear that when we talk about *Dr. Faustus*, we have to clarify which *one* we mean.

As a brief sidebar: textual studies have yielded specific and useful terminology which can be instructive in defining the differences in often incorrectly interchangeably used references. As Sarah Neville notes:

> *Works* are the composition of artists, and different materials produce different forms of art. The constituent element of the literary works produced by authors is language, a medium that, though it can be represented in writing, is fundamentally intangible. [...] A literary *text* is an arrangement or sequence of words that can be materialized in a *document*, the actual artifact containing a piece of writing. (28–29)

We will employ Neville's useful phrasing throughout this volume.

The example of the various *Faustus* texts demonstrates just how much early modern plays evolved, changed, and extended, even long after their authors' deaths.

These conditions ultimately apply to theatres across space and time, up to the moment of two crucial inventions: rapid and easy printing, and copyright law.

To Folio or not to Folio

Shakespeare's First Folio (often designated by scholars as F or F1), published in 1623, is a generally favored origin point for many editions of Shakespeare's plays (although some do prefer other editions: check their notes). Published seven years after Shakespeare's death, in an effort organized by his friends and fellow players, the Folio is a tremendous book, designed and intended for use by readers in homes. It's not a book to carry around in one's pocket. In Shakespeare's lifetime, his plays were printed individually in smaller quarto editions. *Pericles* (1609) and *The Two Noble Kinsmen* (1634) appear only in quarto form. At least 18 of the 38 extant plays were printed individually prior to the Folio's publication, and these early documents often differ considerably from the Folio versions.

These individually published early texts have a great deal of value because they show us a version of the play at a specific point in time. Often, they are shorter than the versions published in the Folio and offer intriguing snapshots into the evolution of early modern plays. Different quartos can show different versions of the play. As noted, the A- and B-Texts of *Dr. Faustus* demonstrate significant differences: the 1616 quarto lacks 36 of the lines in the 1604 quarto, but features 676 new lines. It, additionally, has some interesting subtle variations, such as a shift from "Never too late, if Faustus can repent" to "Never too late, if Faustus will repent" (1616). A small difference on paper, but a tremendous one on stage.

Most famously, the early publication history of *Hamlet* offers intriguing insight into the ways Shakespeare and his contemporaries edited their scripts for particular performance situations. *Hamlet*, besides being Shakespeare's best-known play, boasts a fascinating textual history and appears in multiple formats. Scholar and director Christine Schmidle has done extensive work on early modern German-language translations and adaptations of English plays. She describes *Der Bestrafte Brudermord* (*Fratricide Punished*, printed c.1710) as a shortened, simplified, funnier, translated *Hamlet*, performed by English actors on the continent during Shakespeare's lifetime. More than a decade prior to the publication of Shakespeare's *Hamlet*, we see evidence of a mysterious and now-lost *Ur-Hamlet* (1587). It is often credited to Thomas Kyd, and sometimes to Shakespeare himself, and was a precursor to the version of the play we are familiar with today... eventually. The first published edition of the play appeared almost unrecognizably in quarto form in 1603, potentially released to cash in on the play's popularity. This was cruelly dubbed by early

14 *The Text is a Lie*

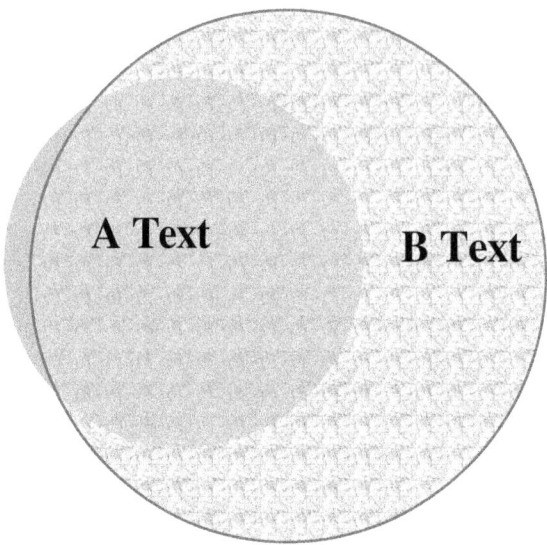

1.3 The A- and B-Texts of *Dr. Faustus* diverge significantly.

scholars as "the Bad Quarto" for its clumsy and unfamiliar phrasing ("To be, or not to be / Ay, there's the point"). It's now more commonly known as "the First Quarto," or Q1. In 1604, this document was almost immediately superseded by an expanded quarto, known now as "the Second Quarto," or Q2, which notes on its title page is based on the "true and perfect Coppie," and which is much more familiar to modern audiences. Almost 20 years later, the play appeared again in revised form in the 1623 Folio. Each of these editions are *markedly* different from one another. Why?

Shakespeare's company performed their plays in the vast space of the Globe and the intimacy of Blackfriars. They toured to town squares and royal palaces. The textual evidence shows his company adapted their scripts for the venue and audience. What we think of today as *Hamlet*—the sprawling, (often) four-hour saga—was likely never performed in its entirety by Shakespeare's own company. The streamlined, unloved Q1 *Hamlet* clocks in at a compact two hours, and is similar in structure, if not in textual detail, to the play Shakespeare's early audiences probably experienced.

Familiarity with this history offers the text cutter both practicality and liberation. Don't feel bound by the text on the page. The authoritative weight of the printed words is, in essence, a lie. We encourage you to free yourself from any concern you may feel of whether this robs your audience of an authentic experience of the play. Cut texts are, in fact, a *more* authentic experience than the behemoth completist text. Further, this sense of how play documents came to be printed and preserved will help you understand the editions we now have available in published form.

Christine Schmidle:
We have the most different versions of *The Spanish Tragedy* (1587) [printed in Europe]. They're all different. We also have *Volpone* (1605) in Germany really early on. We know that the English comedians brought the plays over and performed them right away. We know that there are different versions. We know for sure that the plays went through transformations, because we know how the plays were described. So, for example, with *Romeo and Juliet* (1597), we know the play was performed by different companies, and those companies seemed to have created different versions, as well. In one, Romeo and Paris knew each other, and they got into a fight, and there's another version that is closer to what we know.

1.4 Excerpt from interview with Christine Schmidle, 4 December 2020.

Plays are fragile time travelers

We have certain play documents in multiple forms, others in fragments, and still others merely by reputation or title. The historical plays we think of as exemplary were, in their time, often overshadowed by content modern audiences find impenetrable. The anonymous romantic comedy *Mucedorus* (1590) was the most widely printed play of its time, published in 16 quarto editions, and was wildly popular in performance (Hattaway 129). It's virtually unheard of and unperformed now. Plays that come down to us are a combination of serendipity and design.

Ancient Greek tragedies serve as a fine example. Amy R. Cohen, professor of classics and of theater at Randolph College, shared that documents which survive from that period are mostly those selected for educational purposes. "Certain plays were picked out in the Hellenistic period—in the 3rd and 2nd centuries BCE—as 'these are the plays to teach.' So they got copied more, which is why they got copied enough for at least one copy to survive into the age of monks copying things," she explained. "The plays that got picked for the boys to learn from were not being picked for theatrical success." Another category of Greek play documents, however, survived entirely by accident. The Library of Alexandria had collected many Greek plays, organized in alphabetical scrolls. At the time of the catastrophic fire (48 BCE), the scroll which contained the plays with titles which began with "H" and "I" had been copied enough that those plays survived by random chance. "These plays," Cohen explained, "weren't ones that got picked, it was just that part of the alphabet. I love that because it means we have plays that weren't living up to some particular standard that probably wasn't theatrical."

When we select a document to work from, we must ask, "Where did this come from? Who sent it along to us, from the past? What might have been lost or gained along the way?" Research into the textual history of your script can offer some great options for emendation.

Reasons for cutting

Before we address the process of how we cut a play for modern performance, let's pause to consider cuts or adaptations of plays before our time. Our predecessors' purposes for cuts will often align with our own, and thus inform our path.

Time

First, the plays were condensed for *time*. Theatre is a four-dimensional art form, and the space and time allowed for a production varies based on the context of a given performance. In the Renaissance, plays ran two to three hours, but the specifics depended on the venue. Companies may have had to shorten their performances for events at court, where the play needed to be over by a particular hour so the next item on the schedule would begin on time. An impatient audience might necessitate an expedient cut; the quicksilver-fast surviving copy of *Macbeth* offers evidence of the play-loving yet easily bored King James I's tastes. When Hamlet asks the First Player, "You could, for a need, study a speech of some dozen or sixteen lines, which I would set down and insert in't, could you not?" we can imagine the Player hopes it's not much longer, or he'll need to trim *The Murder of Gonzago* elsewhere in order to get the king to his dinner before it's cold.

Politics

The plays also, through their long performance history, have had both cuts and additions for political reasons. Whether it's an entire scene that makes a ruler uncomfortable, or the excision of a single word that has gained a new and problematic definition since the first version, plays evolve. We can see clear evidence of this evolution in the textual history of *King Lear* and *Hamlet*, both of which demonstrate variance from quarto to Folio. These changes suggest the quarto editions are earlier texts with content which was, for one reason or another, not deemed worthy of inclusion in the Folio. Whether this was a judgment on quality or audience reception is a matter of conjecture. The variance between editions of *King Lear* has been explored exhaustively elsewhere, particularly through a fertile period in the 1980s (see, in particular, Taylor and Warren's *The Division of the Kingdoms*). As this parallel-text example demonstrates, a late scene between Goneril and Albany is much shorter in the Folio, which removes much of Albany's agency and represents a useful example of an early cut.

		Exit Steward.			Enter Albany.
GON	I haue bene worth the whistle.		GON	I have been worth the whistle.	
		Enter the Duke of Albeney.			
ALB	O Gonoril, you are not worth the dust which the winde		ALB	Oh Goneril, You are not worth the dust which the rude wind Blows in your face.	
	Blowes in your face, I feare your disposition, That nature which contemnes it origin, Cannot be bordered certaine in it selfe, She that her selfe will sliuer and disbranch From her materiall sap, perforce must wither, And come to deadly vse.				
GON	No more, the text is foolish.				
ALB	Wisedome and goodnesse to the vilde seeme vilde, Filths sauour but themselues, what haue you done? Tygers, not daughters, what haue you perform'd? A father, and a gracious aged man, Whose reuerence the head-lugd Beare would licke; Most barbarous, most degenerate haue you madded; Could my good brother suffer you to do it? A man, a Prince, by him so beneflicted, If that the heauens do not their visible spirits Send quickly downe to tame the vilde offences, it will come Humanly must perforce prey on it selfe, like monsters of the deepe.				
GON	Milke liuer'd man, That bearest a cheeke for blowes, a head for wrongs, Who hast not in thy browes an eie deseruing thine honour, From thy suffering, that not know'st fooles, do these villains pity Who are punisht ere they haue done their mischiefe. Where's thy drum? France spreds his banners in our noiselesse Land, with plumed helme thy slaier begins threats, Whiles thou a morall foole, sits still and cries Alacke, why does he so?		GON	Milk-liver'd man, That bear'st a cheek for blows, a head for wrongs, Who hast not in thy brows an eye-discerning Thine Honour, from thy suffering.	
ALB	See thy selfe diuell, proper deformity seemes not in the fiend, so horrid as in woman.		ALB	See thy self devil: Proper deformity seems not in the Fiend So horrid as in woman.	
GON	O vaine foole.		GON	Oh vain Fool.	
ALB	Thou chang'd and selfe-couerd thing, for shame Be-monster not thy feature, wer't my fitnesse To let these hands obey my bloud, They are apt enough to dislocate and teare Thy flesh and bones, how ere thou art a fiend, A womans shape doth shield thee.				
GON	Marry your man-hood now ———				
		Enter a Gentleman.			Enter a Messenger.
ALB	What newes?		MESS	Oh my good Lord, the Duke of Cornwall's dead

1.5 Parallel-text analysis reveals gaps not obvious in published editions.

Audiences

Cuts also accommodate different audiences. Tour scripts tend to be both shorter and funnier than those performed in the cities. This was especially true when a tour crossed a language barrier. As Schmidle told us, "It became about telling the story, less in words and more in physicality. Especially in *Hamlet*, the things that just were spoken of and might not have been easily understood, were just cut out." *Hamlet* without soliloquies? In 17th-century Germany, this was the standard version.

Dumb jokes

Sometimes, too, cuts are necessary because, despite the best of intentions from actors and directors alike, 400-year-old humor does not always work. With the right actor and a deep sense of the text, licensed Fools can be riotously funny. But often, as Lear's Fool quips his way through his wordplay or Touchstone doggedly informs us of seven phases of duels, cuts can be merciful. Be careful, though, of too heavy a hand as you judge humor. Often these "unfunny" lines, which were potentially very funny to their original audiences, have specific purposes. This might include a cover for a quick-change, as we see in *As You Like It* (1599), where Touchstone's diatribe allows Rosalind time to change from boy's clothes to girl's clothes. It also gives time to establish character relationships, as we see in *Twelfth Night*. When Feste harangues Viola with one-liners, the funniness is far less central than the interaction.

Clarity

Some cuts are necessary to avoid confusion. *Measure for Measure* can be greatly simplified if you take out a good chunk of the nonsense with the bawds. But don't get ahead of yourself: sometimes what looks like an easy cut is actually a trap. Jonson's *Bartholomew Fair* (1614) is rarely produced today, but when it is, it is a seething mass of characters, intrigues, and wordplay which can leave an audience agog. It may be tempting to trim C- and D-plots, focusing on your central storyline, but those threads can be vital when the piece is up on its feet. Antoni Cimolino, director of a successful *Bartholomew Fair* at Canada's Stratford Festival (2009), confided that his experienced cast was daunted by the weight of the script on the page—until they read it aloud. It suddenly sparkled with life as it returned to the medium for which it was written.

Plays are very much a product of their time, as playwrights comment on society and personalities relevant to the audience. These topical references would have been fun treats for contemporary audiences. When Hamlet greets the players, Rosencrantz informs him they are on tour in part because they

Antoni Cimolino:
[*Bartholomew Fair*] was like: imagine a kaleidoscope. And so to start off, they're gonna go to the fair and they gotta find the reason why: in act one, these Puritans are gonna go to the fair for some pig. And so the different characters come on. And then as the play goes on. He goes from a big long scene in act one to shorter and shorter and shorter scenes in which he takes different characters and he puts them in together and then adds someone else so that your characters have nothing to do with each other. So it's starting to show up, like a green and a blue, and then you turn the kaleidoscope and suddenly there's a pink and blue, and then you turn it again and so… the cutting was really, really delicate because there were so many things [where] you couldn't just say, "I'll take this out," because then you screw the whole play, and yet he's written it so brilliantly. I mean, you know, because he was writing for children. It's kind of actor-proof.

1.6 Excerpt from interview with Antoni Cimolino, 12 February 2021.

are unable to compete with a company of "little eyases," or child actors, a reference which only appears in the Folio. This is an open dig at the competition, variously the Children of Paul's, the Children of the Chapel, and the Children of the Queen's Revels, who leached audiences from Shakespeare's company. In the 17th century, this line might have *killed*. But today? Even the most erudite of audiences will see this as a contemporary reference, a historical nod which engenders no humor whatsoever. Do you cut it because it doesn't help the narrative, and most of your audience won't understand it? Or keep it because it's a historical marker?

The plays of the Restoration and Victorian period are riddled with local references and thinly veiled characters pertinent to a contemporary audience, but utterly impenetrable to audiences today. In John Gay's *The Beggar's Opera* (1728), thieftaker-general Peachum is a thinly disguised parody of British Prime Minister John Walpole in a controversial act of social critique, but 300 years later, this topical reference is immaterial. You might trim these specific references. Be aware, however, that in many of these cases, the detailed digressions are part of the point: Antoni Cimolino discussed Congreve's *Love for Love* (1695) and the difficulty which arises in such an edit, which he described evocatively: "By the time we strip out all of the rich, detailed particular things that make this writer distinct, we've not only reduced the vitamin count, we've actually made it more generic."

Cuts that aren't cuts

In other cases, the lack of cut *is* the cut. Kenneth Branagh's film adaptation of *Hamlet* (1996) was gleefully advertised as the "complete text," due to the fact that it essentially featured every possible line from Q2 and F. It clocked in at 242 minutes, which ultimately necessitated an intermission. Such a choice might be a gesture toward fidelity to the author, but this uncut, cobbled-together version barely resembles anything Shakespeare's company would have recognized. The published play documents were unlikely to have been performed uncut or exactly as-is every time. If you have a version where your cut is the *lack of cut*, be aware it is essentially a *readers' edition*. That's fine. But remember your audience when you do, because the longer it goes, the greater the onus on your quality. Uncut does not equate to "authentic." Nevertheless, Branagh's *Hamlet* was a mighty achievement, and a worthy addition to the Shakespearean film canon, where its "cut" was more to do with arrangement and structure: a "cut" without cuts.

Tim Carroll spoke with us at length about an intentionally uncut production of *Man and Superman*, which included the oft-excised "Don Juan in Hell" third act. Carroll spoke in positive terms of the "extravagance and amplitude" of Shaw's "orgy of words," and the discoveries which came when director Kimberley Rampersad trusted in the completeness of the text. If you have an audience eager to go along with you—as the Shaw Festival did—take full advantage of that luxury.

Cuts across time

Textual cutting is no new phenomenon. After the English theatres closed in 1642, ingenious theatre artists converted the lengthy playhouse-bound scripts into bite-sized cuts, called "drolls," performed in alleys and back rooms during the theatre ban, compact enough to stay a step ahead of the law. Drolls linked scenes from unrelated plays to create new angles on the texts, as Meg Miroshnik evocatively describes in her brilliant dramatization *The Droll (or, a Stage-Play about the END of Theatre)* (2011): "The Droll cuts out / the half-checked bits of JESTERY / from proper Stage-Plays / and just sutures them all together. / Put together a vulgar slice of this and that to make a popular pie." Without this process of excerpts and text cuts, an audience, interrupted mid-scene, would go home dissatisfied and unfulfilled. In a limited amount of time, a five-act dramatic arc was not possible, so the priorities for storytelling shifted to fit the performance conditions. This included new versions of plays developed from the works of Beaumont and Fletcher, Shakespeare, Jonson, Killigrew, and Davenant. Players presented these excerpts, with non-comic sequences erased, with such titles as *The Merry Conceits of Bottom the Weaver* (Taylor 10–11).

A new and incredible period of text-cut industry began when theatres reopened in 1660. The Restoration era and into the 18th century saw sustained interest in the "correction" of old plays through edits. Playwrights like Nahum Tate, George Villiers, David Garrick, John Dryden, and Colley Cibber approached pre-Restoration plays with unbridled glee. They snipped away characters, extended love scenes, elevated villains to heroic levels, and added elements their audiences would like. These new creations include Dryden and D'avenant's *The Enchanted Island* (1670, a version of Shakespeare's *The Tempest*), William Mountfort's farce version of Marlowe's *Dr. Faustus* (1680), Cibber's *Love Makes a Man* (1700, an adaptation of Beaumont and Fletcher's *The Custom of the Country*), and Tate's *Injur'd Love, or, The Cruel Husband* (1707, an adaptation of Webster's *The White Devil*). All were carefully crafted to appeal to Restoration audiences (Clark 289). Several actor-managers of the time, including David Garrick and William Charles Macready, preferred "happy ending" tragedies, where Elizabethan endings were changed for the audience's benefit. This approach to cuts turned classics into entirely new, hugely popular plays. Actor-managers had no reason to approach the plays with reverence, so they adjusted these "old" words to something new audiences would like. They cut with the subtlety of a chainsaw, but provide an important lesson: when you cut without fear, sometimes you can generate an entirely new, vibrant product.

Historically, the cutting of playtexts has been grounded in the reality that these are not immutable, untouchable, totemic objects. By the late 19th century, the vogue became the restoration of cut lines. In 1888, Henry Irving performed *Richard III* with "the original text by Shakespeare" instead of the then-customary Cibber text. As the Victorian reverence for the playwright settled in (dismissed by Shaw as "Bardolatry"), cuts became less fashionable. Through the 20th century, cuts gradually became something of a "dirty little secret," rarely discussed, but often necessary. Indeed, as Bruce R. Smith examines in his indispensable *Shakespeare/Cut*, there has never been a time when text cuts have gone away, even as they have evolved and changed with the rise of new technologies and theatrical movements that focus on abstract modern cuts which fragment and distort the works. Smith's mediation speaks for itself and renders any further exploration on modern cut history moot, but even through his relentless exposure of cut traditions, negative attitudes toward the process have remained. In fact, it might be accurate to say the sense that a cut profanes a "sacred" classic text has grown. We think this stance is worthy of enquiry.

Works cited

Clark, Sandra. "Shakespeare and Other Adaptations." *A Companion to Restoration Drama*, Edited by Susan J. Owen, London: Wiley-Blackwell, 2008, pp. 274–290.

Hattaway, Michael. *Elizabethan Popular Theatre: Plays in Performance*. Theatre Production Studies ser. London: Routledge, 1982.

Neville, Sarah. "1. Editing English Renaissance Texts". *Handbook of English Renaissance Literature*, edited by Ingo Berensmeyer, Berlin and Boston: De Gruyter, 2019, pp. 27–45. https://doi.org/10.1515/9783110444889-002

Rasmussen, Eric. *A Textual Companion to 'Dr Faustus'*. Manchester: Manchester UP, 1993.

Smith, Bruce R. *Shakespeare / Cut: Rethinking Cutwork in an Age of Distraction*. Oxford: Oxford UP, 2016.

Taylor, Gary. *Reinventing Shakespeare: A Cultural History from the Restoration to the Present*. Oxford and New York: Oxford UP, 1991.

Taylor, Gary, and Michael Warren, eds. *The Division of the Kingdoms: Shakespeare's Two Versions of King Lear*. Oxford: Oxford UP, 1987.

2 Start Here
The Three Questions

Once we have finished with the question of whether we should cut and how such cuts have happened in the past, we move into the most operative question of all, which daunts most first-time cutters:

How do I start? *Where* do I start?

No matter what you cut, whether it be your attempt to trim racist language from *Too Much Johnson* (1894) or to reduce *Volpone* to a one-act chamber piece, it is critical you approach the play as a whole object. An objectively strong cut begins with familiarity with the text and with the purpose for each element. As Elinor Fuchs reminds us, "Nothing in the play is without significance" (5). This ought not discourage cutting, but serves as a reminder that every line you cut once had, and likely still has, a *purpose*. It can sometimes be difficult, even painful, to cut around such a purpose. As Tim Carroll sagely noted, "Just because you *can* cut something, doesn't mean you *should*." To omit an Act I character, unaware that they return as a central plot point in Act V, can bring trouble later. Shakespeare half-mentions an unseen youngest brother character in the *very first speech* of *As You Like It*, away at school and irrelevant... until the absent scholar shows up in Act V with a message to save the day. Suddenly, the editor has to scramble to re-insert the third brother. Bullet dodged.

Cutting shouldn't be about dodged bullets and corrected excisions. Rather, it should start with foreknowledge. Before you can cut a single line, you must be familiar with what you've got. Read the play. At *least* three or four times, at varying levels of depth. Arrange to see someone else's production, even on video, although we acknowledge such a step might be anathema to many artists. Don't steal their cut, by any means, but pay attention to where you feel lost, bored, or confused. This is a valuable guide as you create a clear story for your audience.

Many of the experts we spoke with described their introduction to cuts through examination of others' work. Martine Kei Green-Rogers remembered her first cut at the Oregon Shakespeare Festival, where then-literary manager Lue Douthit pointed her to the archive of previous cuts: "[Lue told me:] 'You can look at past productions of *A Midsummer Night's Dream*, and use those to think about how you're going to do this.' So this is what I did. I looked at all of these other versions and learned what they did, and then created my own ideal version." Grant Mudge, Ryan Producing Artistic Director at the Notre Dame Shakespeare Festival, describes a similar process. Tasked with a tight cut of *Much Ado About Nothing*, he meticulously transcribed Kenneth Branagh's film cut, pausing the video as he marked up his Riverside Shakespeare. He staged it to figure out what worked, and why. Many years later, he asks his students to cut scenes and compare them to the cuts in Steve Gooch's *The Cut Shakespeare*.

> I have them take the same scene, evaluate his cuts and, as Hugh Cruttwell would say, 'Attend to the disparity' between yours and his. They simply say what they thought was successful about his cut and what wasn't. Then they have to produce their own. This leads to a keen awareness that if you're going to leave a couplet dangling, there better be a damn good reason, and they essentially learn to apply it to any cuts they are making. *Why are you doing it? How does it serve the play, your audience, your actors?*

What is integral? What taps into your design concept? Who feels extraneous? Do you know *why* you're cutting? Is it for time? Clarity? Sense? Company efficiency? If you have a good sense of what you want to do, you will have better clarity later in what you remove.

Major considerations: the Three Questions

The first three pieces of information which define any cut are:

1 Who is my audience?
2 What is my story?
3 How much time do I have?

Every other decision hinges on these three questions.

Question 1: Who is my audience?

As anyone who has ever toured will tell you: every audience is different. It changes depending on whether you're in the city or the country, whether you're uptown or downtown, whether you're outdoors or in. Cultured festival audiences will receive a play very differently from high school students—and not necessarily "better." Be aware who your anticipated audience is.

The Spanish Siglo de Oro plays were written with the knowledge that all classes would converge to watch them, which explains their scintillating combination of high- and low-brow humor sandwiched together. Today, audiences are far less integrated: to momentarily trade in cultural assumptions, a theatre which charges $99 a seat is unlikely to attract as many working-class patrons for a production of *She Stoops to Conquer* (1773) as you might hope.

James Evans:
It's just about clarity, for me. I don't want to smooth out the text. I want ambiguity to live within it, especially a production of *Hamlet*. Hamlet is so ambiguous and completely a contradiction to himself, time and time again…I wanted all of that to sing. But sometimes it's about excising just two lines from a speech that will allow an audience to hear it a bit more clearly. Sometimes in those long, winding parenthetical phrases, I'm always just thinking, "What will the audience hear, what will the audience understand of this?" Rather than, "What are the good bits that I like as a Shakespeare nerd?"

2.1 Excerpt from interview with James Evans, 1 February 2021.

A free lunchtime park production of *The Frogs* (405 BCE) might attract curious passers-by, who care not a whit for the title but are amused by something active, cheap, and convenient to them.

Ask yourself a few basic questions.

What is your audience like?

Many of these questions may yield easy answers, and if you're familiar with your company and audience this may be a simple mental checklist. When you work with a new company or community, it is always useful to check on these facts.

What are their demographics?

How old are they? If you perform for a group of elementary school students, you'd better not cut any physical comedy; if they are old enough to have memorized famous speeches in school, you might think twice before you monkey with those. This question might be tough to answer specifically: after all, we hope to attract people of all walks of life, but it can be useful to gain a general sense of the kinds of people your theatre expects to serve. Neglecting audience demographics might lead to a cut your audience objects to, or which does not fulfill their expectations. Your 35-minute Brechtian deconstruction of *Die Weber* (1892) might be an avant-garde festival hit but be received with distinctly less enthusiasm in a retirement village rec room.

What is their level of familiarity with the play, playwright, historical period, or genre?

In most of the English-speaking world, we can assume an adult audience has some familiarity with the greatest hits of the Western Canon. This might include Sophocles, Shakespeare, Wycherley, Wilde, Ibsen, Shaw, and Chekhov.

In many cases, your audience will recognize the plays, even if they don't know them well ("I've *heard of* the Restoration…"), while they may have studied others in high school ("All I remember about *Hedda Gabler* is falling asleep in class"). Many playwrights are in the cultural groundwater. Freud brought the Oedipal Complex into mainstream vernacular. Any image of a young man under a balcony evokes *Romeo and Juliet*. The rule of "Chekhov's gun" is known to any neophyte screenwriter. Iconic phrases pepper our discourse, from memes to sitcoms to Broadway musicals, and so for a select cross section of works, you can rely somewhat on cultural knowledge. But how well do audiences really know the play? What if they're elementary school children? Or people whose culture includes little to no familiarity with the work? Or people who might have some context on *Antigone* (441 BCE) but none for *Cyclops* (c.412 BCE)? What if you're cutting a playwright your audience has not heard of at all? *Your* familiarity might not match your audience's. As Lue Douthit noted, "My assumption was that everybody knows *Macbeth*, and they don't."

Why are they coming to your show?

Again, it depends on where your theatre is and its standing in the community. Whether your primary demographic is families who want to enjoy a picnic in the park while they catch some light entertainment, or your theatre tour is an annual summer highlight for a small village on the route, this will impact your cut. An audience with hopes for a casual night out is best served by a cut that elides problematic plot points; an audience full of students on a campus trying to process some recent trauma may benefit from a cut which leans into those same scenes to create time and space for their questions.

> **Martine Kei Green-Rogers:**
> If we're doing a cut for an academic audience, one of the first things we want to think about is, what are we trying to teach the students? What are the student learning outcomes? Is it about wrestling with the language? Is it about figuring out how the comedy of Chekhov works? What is the thing that we are trying to get them to do? What do we want our audiences to take away, and how do we want them to understand the work? It isn't necessarily the same concerns as one would have in a professional setting. There might be a particular joke that has run its course and yet is in there several times. In a professional setting, you might let one go, but if you're trying to teach students things like comic timing, you might leave it in.

2.2 Excerpt from interview with Martine Kei Green-Rogers, 28 January 2021.

Take Ira Aldridge's *The Black Doctor* (1847). Fabian, the titular doctor, confesses his love for Pauline, a white aristocratic woman, on a remote beach as the tide rises. He says his plan is they will both die together, since it is impossible for them to marry. In this play, by a Black man, about a Black man, the character choices are distressing and complicated. In some audience contexts, this is exactly why we would produce this play. In others, perhaps we would cut as follows, to make Fabian's actions less horrifying.

PAULINE: (*rising agitated, looks at the sea, which is gradually surrounding them*) Fabian! Fabian! Not now; the sea rises. Let us go. Come, come, Fabian!

FABIAN: (~~detains her~~) Go! (*smiles*) No, ~~the mulatto had calculated every chance; in his turn he had deceived the young girl—he had led her into a snare~~—they both stood here—on the spot we now occupy; the tide was rising fast, only one path was free—but the sea continued to gain on them (*seizes both her hands*). ~~The young girl entreated the mulatto to try to save her; but he, without pity for her terror or her tears, held her with hands of iron.~~ At last, he told her he loved her (*looking round*). Still the sea was gaining ground; every chance of escape was gone, and yet death has less of horror for the young girl than the mulatto's love.

PAULINE: (*in much terror*) Fabian, for pity's sake, save me!

FABIAN: Save you! And is it not possible you guess I love you?

PAULINE: (*struggling with her feelings*) No, no! You are deceiving me; you would not—could not see me die here before your eyes!

FABIAN: (*pointing to sea*) Look, Pauline, before we should reach the rocks which we now but descended together, the sea would dash us to atoms against their rugged points! ~~I feared my own weakness, and closed every avenue to the road of repentance or pity;~~ death surrounds us, but we shall perish together! ~~How! You no longer tremble, will you not call down heaven''s curses on your destroyer''s head?~~

PAULINE: (*solemnly*) Fabian!

FABIAN: (*pointing to sea*) No earthly power can save us!

PAULINE: (*rushing to pathway, which the sea has not yet reached*) Then let me beg my mother's forgiveness and pray to heaven for you (*falls on her knees against the rock*).

FABIAN: For me!

PAULINE: Yes, for you! Now I am sure of death, I may acknowledge, without shame or remorse, that I understand you, Fabian, and I forgive you, for I have long, long loved you!

FABIAN: Did I hear aright? Love me! ~~And I—I am her murderer!~~ Oh, heavens, (*rushes to her and supports her in his arms*) you will not allow it! Kill me! But save her! (*looks around*) Ah! 'Tis too late! She is already dying.

That cut is the difference between a romantic comedy and a complex story of individual abuse as a response to systemic abuse. The play is not as interesting this way, but many audiences might prefer it for their date night.

What is their relationship to theatre?

Does your audience have a pre-existing relationship to theatre, or is this new to them? You may assume people less familiar with theatre are unlikely to welcome an adventurous production, but often, a lack of preconceptions creates space for experimentation. If you anticipate your audience is familiar with theatre, or the specific works of your playwright, consider whether they are interested in being surprised and challenged, or would prefer to see exactly what they expect.

Theatrical norms in the modern Western world generally require audiences to sit in darkness, the attentive silence disturbed only by the crinkle of candy wrappers or the occasional unfortunate cellphone. This is not the only way to enjoy a play. In many past times and places, audiences came to the theatre to chat with friends, buy oranges and prostitutes, flirt, notice who was there and with whom. The play could be incidental, at best, as audiences tuned in and out of the story. Imagine the atmosphere at a stadium, or in a bar where there's live music.

Playwrights knew they couldn't depend on their audience's rapt attention, so carefully repeated plot points, mentioned character names every time they entered, and frequently recapped anything crucial to understanding the next portion of the action. If your audience is conventionally quiet and focused, repeated phrases and clauses help with comprehension and clarity, but can also be redundant and easy to cut. With an inexperienced audience, however, such a decision removes some vital tools which can make or break how they understand the narrative. Move too fast, and your audience might get lost, which then means they might get restless. Or go home. On the other hand, if you cut more adventurously for a Festival audience familiar with the play, you run the risk of alienating purists. It is a tightrope act.

Is the audience familiar with your company? You can leverage this in a number of ways. If they have seen your actors before, they might be better

---

Martine Kei Green-Rogers:
It takes a while for our aural self to be able to sink into the language. I think it's important that you're not cutting with a contemporary ear. Some of the repetition that is embedded in Shakespeare because of the structures in which Shakespeare was presenting work—the noisiness that was the Globe—some of that repetition can go, yes, but if it's in the top of the play, maybe you should leave it. That gives people the opportunity to be able to hear the language and slide into the early modern English without having to worry if they missed something important because their brains didn't click into it immediately.

2.3 Excerpt from interview with Martine Kei Green-Rogers, 28 January 2021.

able to remember faces and follow their stories. You might not need so much repetition.

Are you about to cut the work of a playwright who is a major box-office draw for audiences, or are your audiences likely less familiar with their work? An audience familiar with the playwright's oeuvre will need their hands held far less. Even in plays they haven't seen, they will rely on conventions they've learned from the playwright's other work. You will be able to cut more liberally and expect them to follow the story anyway.

What will make them tell their friends to come see you next weekend? Word of mouth is the best kind of marketing, so you want to send them home energized and excited. An over-long drag of a play won't have this effect, but neither will one that leaves them befuddled. Unfamiliar plays require a clear cut to bring forward the key elements of the story; for well-known plays, the best cuts show the audience something they hadn't recognized before.

What do they expect to see?

What does your audience expect to see when they come to your theatre? To what extent do you want to serve or challenge their expectations? Producing art is always a balance between stretching your audience and encouraging them to return. Stretch them too far, and they won't return. Stretch them too little, and they'll see your productions as predictable and therefore skippable. If you are in a theater you aren't familiar with, ask someone who knows the audience well *why* they attend. You may be surprised to discover what you assumed to be a complacent older audience are actually 1960s revolutionaries who have barely mellowed as they've aged. Stereotypes are dangerous; check in with real experience.

How long are typical performances in this theatre? What is expected? What is beyond the pale? If your company routinely asks audiences to enjoy three-hour performances, you may not need to worry about the time crunch as much. By the same token, however, that three-hour audience might not look kindly on a one-hour supercut, so figure out what your audience and company can handle.

It is always fruitful to attempt to know what the audience expects, whether or not you choose to work to that. If you're with an established company, one of the most instructive questions to ask is, "What was a production you thought was great, but your audience *hated*?"

Question 2: What is my story?

The second of the three questions revolves around a reminder: every cut should clarify the story you want to tell. In this sense, the term "story" is both broad and specific. The editor should work with clarity on the whole-play story, but within that larger story exist smaller narratives to construct the world of the play. Consider not just the story of the play, but also the stories of the characters. Within the play's bounds, the information we have is dictated by multiple character stories as they come together. Strindberg's *Miss Julie* (1889) may, on the macro level, drive toward Julie's loss of status, but it also tells the story of Jean, and, third, the story of Christine. There is the story of Julie's father, the story of his estate, and the story of the Midsummer's Eve revels. It is a story of class and a story of power. There are many stories, and on the simplest level, we can break a play down as each character requires a clearly defined arc. Every act has a story. Every scene has a story. Plays are story-fractals.

When you make cuts, especially large cuts, question whether your cuts serve the story(ies).

The first rule is, the story is where you find it. The dramatic canon comprises a wealth of texts which feature a great many different stories which wait inside them. This is why we can watch the same plays over and over, and yet never see the same show twice.

The Importance of Being Earnest (1895) features many possible stories. Here is a sample:

- A love story between a man and his beloved, despite the presence of her domineering mother.
- A caustic commentary on Victorian social structures, which includes how gossip, innuendo, and societal expectations impact relationships.
- An encoded, extended male friendship designed to appeal to a society accustomed to necessarily-hidden masculine love.
- A conversation on identity and its place in society, and the ways meaning is ascribed without explicit intent.
- A pointed critique of the Anglican church and educational reform.

All of these stories exist within *The Importance of Being Earnest*, along with many more.

Each of these stories can be integral to the plot of your play. Sometimes, you can place them in the background, ignore them, or omit them. While pieces of them can coexist, they differ vastly in who has agency to move the story forward. Each separate story ascribes different motives to characters. A focus on a *particular* story, ideally based on your prior knowledge of your audience and the production company's goals, might mean other stories can step back. When they step back, cuts are more likely to be successful. We should never forget that even though we have established this ideal of siloing stories into distinct piles, stories will interlace and tendrils will reach from one story to another. You could minimize the "story" of Princess Glauce from *Medea* (431 BCE), but too much undercuts Creon's and Jason's story. Cut with care.

Every act is a web of possible stories, as is every scene. Keep track of the stories of these scenes, as this can guide your cut. Write a brief summary of each act and scene, and use those as a test to determine what gets cut and what stands.

Lue Douthit:
One of the things I do, and this is something I've been doing for a long time, is that I chart all the plays [of Shakespeare] and kind of know how they work. Because my theory is, if you don't know how the play works in a certain proportion, I don't know how you're going to cut it. Listen, if you got time, you got to know how to play works, not necessarily what the play is about. I'm not so sure you're really in charge of that as a director, honestly. But if you think that you have to know how to ride those rails, you have to know how the rails work.

2.4 Excerpt from interview with Lue Douthit, 24 February 2021.

You may find it helpful to create a visualization of the whole play for yourself, as well, in diagrams, charts, or heat maps. If you map the events of the play onto a tool like Freytag's Pyramid, which is based around lessons codified in Aristotle's *Poetics* (335 BCE), you can clarify the story, reduced to its simplest components:

1. Exposition
2. Inciting incident
3. Rising action
4. Climax
5. Falling action
6. Resolution

Will the focus of your production change these core elements? Plan how, before you commence.

If your story for the final act of *Hamlet* centers on Hamlet's growing awareness of mortality, you wouldn't cut big chunks of his graveyard musings, as he personifies bones and chats to Yorick. On the other hand, if you were to build the story around the grief-stricken madness of Hamlet and Laertes, you might slice the Gravedigger sections to bits to allow time and space for their fight over Ophelia's body.

Lastly, every character is on a journey through their play. As imaginative and industrious directorial concepts have proven over and over again, in most plays, characters are open to a range of interpretations. If you plan a clear story for each character before you begin to cut, you avoid accidentally erasing crucial details of the character's journey. Oswald's journey through *Ghosts* is built around multiple stories: his past, his father, his feelings for Regine, and his ambitions for the future. Emphasis on one story over the others changes the story of the production, rendering it an indictment of

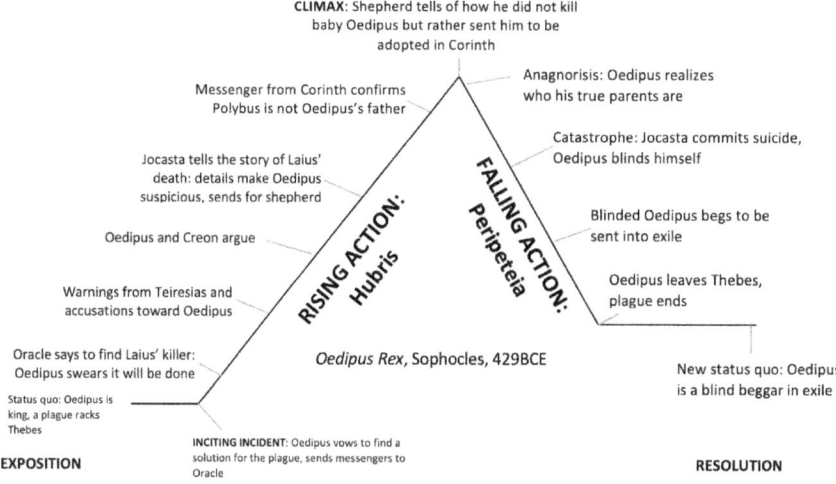

2.5 Freytag's Pyramid, applied to Sophocles' *Oedipus Rex*.

Mrs. Alving's deception or an examination of Engstrand's true character. The editor has the opportunity to decide which stories lie at the emphatic point in their production. Christine Schmidle, reflecting on her work at Shakespeare's Globe, recounted that the one thing she always checks for when she reviews cuts is that each character's journey is complete: "We make sure that Malvolio has his insult to Feste early on, because it comes back at the end and completes that story." It's easy to miss, if you cut from the beginning of the script without a holistic view, but is crucial to resolving *Twelfth Night*'s B-plot.

Question 3: How much time do I have?

It won't surprise you to discover that this is the point which often interests audiences most. We should listen to the groans which greet a theatre program's cheerful announcement: *"Tonight's performance will run for three hours (without intermission)."* We are absolutely convinced of the importance of lines which have survived long enough to come down to us over hundreds of years of performance and publication, yet there is a special kind of masochism in companies who doggedly perform classical drama uncut, as some kind of endurance test.

Practical constraints often determine runtime. Sometimes you need to finish before the last subway train stops for the night, or before a certain hour nudges unionized crew into overtime. Sometimes you perform for teenagers on a field trip and you only have an hour. Whatever it is, if you begin with a predetermined artificial timeframe, you cut to fit within it, rather than the opposite process, which is to cut as you need and test the length of what you have.

Believe it or not, a time frame can be a happy constraint. With a finite period, you can undertake more brutal cuts than you might without limitation. Think of it as a bookshelf: once your bookshelf is full, you cannot add any more books to your collection unless you select an item on the shelf to replace. This strict limitation encourages you to justify the presence of every line and story. Does it earn its place on the "shelf"?

Every cutter has their own metric to estimate time: Lue Douthit shared how her former colleague Scott Kaiser calculated "a formula that's pretty scarily accurate: number of words, which includes character names, as well as stage directions, divided by 135, will give you the minutes it will take to perform. It's scary how close it is."

The American Shakespeare Center (Staunton, VA), has a house style with tight pacing. This is crucial to how they calculate stage time. Their actor training emphasizes a classical technique with very few breaks in the text and rapid, clear speech. With such a group of actors, line delivery clocks in at around 20 lines per minute (LPM).

Understand that speed should never be at the expense of clarity, as Tina Packer noted. For her work at Shakespeare & Company (Lenox, MA), actors practice a similarly swift execution: "We do like to go very fast in performance, but not before everybody knows exactly what they're saying and indeed are experiencing what they're saying while they're saying it, so it's never reported speech. It is *created* speech." That said, the faster you go, the less you have to cut.

If you work with less experienced actors, or employ a style that allows for more silence, you might more realistically estimate 15 lines per minute.

This range can make a huge difference.

Ralph Alan Cohen:
I never have given a note in my life, telling an actor to speed up. Ever. I am mostly telling them to go from 78 RPM all the way past 45 down to 33 RPM, get it down to 33, but make up for that by hitting your cues, and don't screw around. [I saw a student scene from *Love's Labour's Lost* where they put a ladder on stage]. When Berowne goes to say his kind of cap thing, he's going to end the scene at the top of the ladder. He stops talking to climb the ladder. Then he does the speech. In my production, he would figure out that he could climb the ladder and talk at the same time. That's where I think you make up the time. I don't believe in pauses. If the actor's not in a spotlight to keep your attention, you'll look someplace else, so Shakespeare needed someone to be talking.

2.6 Excerpt from interview with Ralph Alan Cohen, 24 November 2020.

Elizabeth Cary's *Miriam, Queen of Jewry* (1613) is 2269 lines long. If your actors run at 20 LPM, this totals about 113 minutes. On the other hand, the same play spoken at 15 LPM comes in at 151 minutes. Half an hour is an eternity in the theatre. Pacing matters.

You can generally calculate modern prose plays at roughly a page per minute, but time by line-count works best for verse dramas, which includes the works of the Ancient Greeks and the Elizabethans. Verse takes longer to speak than quippy one-liners, and different genres necessitate different styles. Comedies may zip along at a quicker pace than a more languid drama, but must account for laughs and audience interaction. Sometimes the best way to test a play's length is to read it aloud. The ideal situation is to gather a group of actors to do a read-through so you can hear it, but this is not a luxury available at all times. Instead, just try it yourself, and play all the roles. Take a speech or a segment, read it at the pace you would in performance, and count how many lines you speak in a minute. It might be fewer than you think.

If you are able to peruse past cuts and performance times for your company, a little math will get you in the right neighborhood. One fun way to estimate pace is to remember (or watch a video of) an actor from the company as they perform a monologue. This should give you a sense of their style as it will translate to the performance. Now. Cast your mind back to the golden hits of American radio. An experienced, confident actor might hit the rhythm of the speech at a tempo matching the pace of Gloria Gaynor's 1978 disco anthem "I Will Survive." That rhythm comes in at one hundred beats per minute, which, given a five-beat verse line, is 20 LPM. On the other hand, a less experienced or more languid performer might deliver the same speech with a slower cadence, say, along the lines of Elvis Presley's 1957 "All Shook Up" (Are you humming yet?). This slower pace indicates this performer can handle around 15 LPM. We don't want to ask actors to speed up in order to hit a time limit: this can damage a lot of great work between actors and directors. You should construct your script to give the company the best possible shot at success.

In general, a more conservative time estimate is better. If you're not sure, just assume 15 verse LPM (or 150 syllables per minute). If your show ends up shorter than you'd hoped, you can add in an extra song, lengthen a fight scene, or give an actor back a monologue you had slashed. Confiscating lines once actors own them is much harder.

Published editions of classical early modern verse documents often feature line numbers, provided by helpful editors. This might seem a useful shortcut for estimating your line count, but these line numbers are often inconsistent. Some editors count half-lines or divided lines as one line or multiple, which you should pay attention to, as this can skew line estimates.

Prose, on the other hand, is trickier. Without the same page layout, prose lines tend to be longer than verse lines, since typesetters fit as many words as they can on a single line. An actor usually takes a lot longer to speak ten lines of prose than ten lines of verse. If your play is prose-heavy, assume two lines of prose count as roughly one verse line.

If this all seems like a lot of boring and tedious math, it definitely is. It frustrated Aili so much she developed software tools to mark cuts, calculate runtimes, and share marked-up and cleaned-up scripts with a production team. These tools generate scene charts and warn you if you have an actor onstage as two characters at once. To learn more about these tools, please visit us at www.cuttingplays.com.

In addition to the text, you will need to account for *business*, or additional non-textual onstage action which takes up time and space beyond what is printed on the page. This includes songs, dances, battles, entrances, fights, and artistic transitions. Leave enough padding so your fight choreographer and dance captain have room to work. A to-the-second, letter-perfect cut will likely run overtime after the added impact of live actors. Know how much time your fight choreographer thinks the big battle will take *before* you get too committed to your cut. If they have cinematic visions, you might have to sacrifice some bits of wit.

Lastly, remember that time matters in practical ways for actors. Read through the play and follow each actor's track. Think about whether they will have sufficient time both for logistical concerns, like costume changes, and narratological concerns. Think about whether there's enough time for the story to make sense. Aili once made a cut in *Antony and Cleopatra* she came to regret. After Antony receives (false) news of Cleopatra's death, he quickly decides he needs to follow her. Aili's cut removed eight lines from this already too-short moment, which caused actor Scott Lange to joke, "Since Cleopatra died—30 seconds ago—I have lived in such dishonor that the gods detest my baseness." The removed lines made what was already a challenge for the actor significantly harder. Theatre is a four-dimensional art form; be careful when you mess with time.

Asked and answered

The Three Questions are a tool to help you understand what you have, and should be a given before you cut a syllable. Often, a number of close readings and consideration of context leads to preservation of speeches or moments which earlier felt like easy cuts. Once you've asked these Three Questions, and worked them through, you are ready to gather your materials and take a first tentative step toward shaping the play to what you need it to be.

Works cited

Gooch, Steve. *The Cut Shakespeare.* https://www.stevegooch.info/thecut/
Freytag, Gustav. *Freytag's Technique of the Drama: An Exposition of Dramatic Composition and Art.* Ed. Elias J. MacEwan. Chicago: Scott, Foresman and Company, 1900.
Fuchs, Elinor. "EF's Visit to a Small Planet: Some Questions to Ask a Play." *Theater* 34:2, pp. 5–9. https://doi.org/10.1215/01610775-34-2-5

3 The Cutter's Toolkit Part One
Materials

Once you have a good handle on your script, you are ready to begin your first cut. As you cut, think about the following elements, which act as essential items and options within any cutter's toolkit. You may not use all of them all the time, but you'll be glad to have the option. Begin a cut without a plan or the correct tools and you will find the process a slog. This chapter represents a toolkit, compiled as a comprehensive, non-exhaustive guide: a collection of tools we collectively cannot do without when we start a cut, both in terms of physical items and useful resources.

Before you start: a moment of reassurance

As we assembled this volume, we interviewed 19 highly skilled text cutters from across three continents, many of whom cut for some of the highest-profile theatre organizations in the English-speaking world. We began each interview with a simple question:

"How did you learn to cut?"

The answers were not only illuminating, but were almost all a variation on a theme. Bestselling author and (intentionally) uncredited text editor for the Public Theater's Shakespeare in Central Park, James Shapiro, whom one might expect to be classically trained in the process, surprised us with the opposite fact. Indeed, he confided: "I had no experience doing this: someone told me they needed a 90-minute cut," so he just… figured it out. We heard the same story over and over. Expert cutters described their initiation as being "thrown in the deep end" (Kate Mulvany), "a journey of a thousand mistakes" (Megan McDonough), "learned on the fly" (Tina Packer), and "trial by fire" (James Evans). Both Lue Douthit and Martine Kei Green-Rogers spoke of the value in the Oregon Shakespeare Festival Archives, where cuts of predecessors instructed theirs. Similarly, Antoni Cimolino would point directors to the Stratford Festival Archives for cut guidance, and noted one director returned with some consternation, as he noticed past productions were so influential, "everyone kept the same things." Both Aili and Toby share exactly the same experience. Some interviewees spoke of mentorship, but not one learned cut mechanics in a classroom or formal seminar.

DOI: 10.4324/9781003160076-4

The point is: don't let the cut intimidate you. The only way to start is to dive in (but keep in mind the rigorous preparation steps we have already described!) and remember: your first cut is nearly never your final one. It will take time, and focus, and many revisions, but there is no way to hedge in the outset. You will learn things about yourself, your process, and what works for this particular script, and you will adjust. And adjust again. In the process you'll get to know your play, inside and out. As James Shapiro noted: "This work has made me a much better scholar." Let's get started!

Physical materials: texts and stationery

Your physical approach to materials will be entirely personal. You may want to experiment with different methods. The authors diverge significantly. Aili prefers to cut on screen to easily track line count and share with collaborators. Toby only ever cuts on paper, which can be fiddly, but offers a welcome tactile sensation and catharsis when the cut is transferred into a computer file. Both cut with as good a peer-reviewed edition of the text as we can find: an Arden Shakespeare, or a Yale Sophocles. A New Mermaid Jonson. In a pinch, a Dover Thrift Ibsen or a Signet Wilde will do the job, but you want an edition on hand you can refer to for guidance. Our interviewed artists declared their dedication to a range of editions, depending on how they prioritize format and annotation.

Approach internet editions of plays with caution, because they often lack any indication of editorial intervention or attribution. A play listed on Archive.org or Project Gutenberg might be absolutely sound, so long as you're aware you might miss context on textual variance or irregularities. You might seek a peer-reviewed online text, such as the comprehensive texts at the Theoi Classical Texts Library, Queen's Men Editions, Digital Renaissance Editions, Folger Shakespeare, and Internet Shakespeare Editions, which feature variant texts, annotations, and primary sources. Other sites exist with useful resources, such as Wilde Online, and the MIT Shakespeare, but these do not include annotations or editorial apparatus useful in pre-production. All of these resources are listed in our appendices.

Peer-reviewed editions have thorough annotations, where the editor's in-depth notes and insight might help you make a decision. It is very useful to include a peer-reviewed edition and its editorial notes with your preparation. You may even choose to complete your cut *in* your edition, but this makes annotations difficult (and rearrangement impossible without scissors) in what are usually very small margins.

Have a reliable pencil (or if you're bold, pen) so any strikethroughs of cut text can still be read under the line. Cutters often excise a line and think better of it on a second read, so don't obliterate the line, at least not yet. We have, on more than one rookie occasion, learned the perils of cuts with a Sharpie.

If you cut on screen—say, for example, you have converted your downloaded Project Gutenberg copy of *Dr. Faustus* into a Word document to

> **James Shapiro:**
> The very first thing I do: I go to the Folger Shakespeare site, where I can download an HTML version of the text that I want. I was on the board of governors at the Folger and I fought very hard when I was overseeing the scholarly affairs committee, to get them to release their text so that it would supplant the MIT text, which is the old 19th-century Globe Shakespeare that is riddled with errors, that I had to use at the beginning of my career. So the first thing to do, as a rule, is to go to the Folger site and to download a free copy of the text, which is an outstanding text. I don't agree with everything, and every now and then I will make variants between Q and F, but that's what I do.

3.1 Excerpt from interview with James Shapiro, 8 February 2021.

edit—we advise you resist the delete key, at least for now. You are far better off to use a highlighter tool or strikethrough formatting to indicate what you are removing. This will give you a better sense of the structure of the words on the page, will indicate cut proportions, and can be easily reversed. Even after you are certain your cut is complete, don't get rid of the version of the script which shows what you've cut. We both did this at the outset of our careers and lived to regret it later. Sometimes a director wants to know exactly what you cut from the prologue. Sometimes you want to compare your cut with a colleague's, and this is more complicated without the struck-through words. Make a copy to fully excise the cuts, but keep your marked-up text somewhere safe.

Keep in mind the limitations you have set out for yourself in regards to audience, story, and time: this should offer a strong sense of your goals. While it might feel overly cautious to clarify these specifics before you take scissors to a text, this is preferable to cuts for the wrong reasons.

However you approach it, you want space to work. Often, a cut goes through multiple formats, from paperback to printout to a digital document and back again. Pencil allows for easy erasure, but ultimately, work in a format which makes sense to *you*.

Lexicons and dictionaries and variorums, oh my!

You should seek out materials for your cut which include resources to make your life easier. This might include scholarship, or reference materials, to help you understand hidden clues in your play. The internet has made research infinitely more accessible. A quick Google search or access to the Oxford English Dictionary online can illuminate an obscure word or its historical usage. Don't feel you have to undertake this challenge alone: these reference materials will support your work and will help you justify a cut or a preservation of text.

For any cutter, clarity is paramount, so if you take on Ibsen or Sophocles or Jonson, and don't understand what a word or moment means, it's crucial you take the time to understand its function in the play before you simply cut it. Something which seems difficult, arbitrary, and cuttable might be foundational, as Megan McDonough related to us. She once cut the dream sequence from *Cymbeline*, feeling that it was extraneous, which led to major complications in the final concept of the play. Seek out research and scholarship, use secondary sources as they are available, and get to know your play, inside and out. We have listed some useful resources at the end of the book and on www.cuttingplays.com.

Physical materials: visualization

How will you visualize your cut? Sometimes, the 10,000-foot view of the cut can be instructive. Each cutter we interviewed had their own way to visualize their cut, which included diagrams, maps, sketches, and software. Both Toby and Aili have particular quirks with text visualization which build on our own personal interests.

Toby, for example, places all texts in a Microsoft Excel spreadsheet, with one cell per line of text. As he cuts lines, he leaves the negative space behind, to make gaps in the cut clear. As he completes subsequent cuts, he adds new columns, building a visual map of the progress of the script. For example, a series of cuts of *Henry the Sixth, Part One* is visualized over a series of eight separate cuts, with instances of a heavy cut (on the right) and a moderate cut (on the left), which evolved through rehearsals (see Figure 3.2). Parallel-text editions are a good way to visualize the evolution of your script, in case there is a need to return to a prior cut. This is a user-friendly approach to text, in easy-to-access software.

Aili's custom-built software dynamically shows and hides cuts, highlights and color-codes characters' lines, and even allows her to follow the track of a single character through the play via part-scripts. She likes using these tools because they cut down on repetition of work and they facilitate the parts of the cutting process—like endlessly recounting lines—that she finds tedious. They also offer a great deal of flexibility sharing scripts with collaborators, allowing them to adjust the text to work with their own processes.

Copy text: editions and texts

Here we wade into the weeds, where artists and academics often part ways. *Often*, but not always. You may not have thought much about the origin of your script. To the young actor or inexperienced director, textual history is the least of their concerns. To cut a play, surely it's as simple as this: *grab a copy from the shelf or the internet and attack it, right?* Not quite.

3.2 This parallel-text approach demonstrates the textual evolution of a play over the course of the process.

Edition selection can have a profound impact on your production and the story you want to tell. While your audience may not care whether you've used the Arden, Penguin, or Cambridge, the *edition* choice sends a specific message to your company about the way you will approach the play. The *text* of the play? That's a whole other matter.

A quick refresher on the difference between "*edition*" and "*text*": The "*edition*" you may work from is *the published script*: your Penguin, your Yale Press, your Everyman. This (almost always) features some form of editorial intervention, where an editor has applied (often peer-reviewed) informed choices to what text should appear where. This extends to formatting, stage directions, and, in select instances, *textual variance*. The "*text*" of the play speaks to this textual variance, or variant line readings for the same play, which sometimes (but not always) exist due to publication of multiple versions of texts. To return to Sarah Neville: the text is "an arrangement or sequence of words that can be materialized in a *document*" (in this case the specific edition), which by definition means that this sequence is subject to change between editions. This could be due to translation, in-performance alteration, or authorial change. Alternate versions of your play may exist, and if they do, you should consider them. Textual variants are most famously demonstrated in the Early Modern publication industry. As we've discussed, many early plays appeared individually, often in quarto format, small books made from large sheets of paper folded into quarters.

More prestigiously, some playwrights, such as Jonson and Shakespeare, had their works collated into handsome, expensive Folios, made from sheets of paper folded only once. As these editions featured reprints of previously published plays, we may note variance between texts. This is because published plays were often revised and republished, which resulted in two versions. Jonson's *Every Man in His Humour* changed markedly between the 1601 Q1 and the 1616 Folio. Many of Shakespeare's plays, such as *Romeo and Juliet*, *Othello*, *King Lear*, and *Hamlet* vary wildly between published texts.

When a scholar sets out to edit an academic edition of a play, they will consider every permutation of the text, and base their edition primarily on one particular text: this is known as the *copy text*. An editor who oversees a new edition of Beaumont's *The Knight of the Burning Pestle* (1613) might see interesting details in the 1679 Second Folio and choose to make it the copy text, which means they accept F2 as the baseline text unless they see something more useful in another edition. The editor flags this variance for the reader, as we discuss below.

When we use "copy text" in the context of this guide, we apply it in the same way: a baseline text on which you build your cut. This could be an edited edition or an early quarto or Folio. There's no wrong way: the edited copy will feature useful guidance from an expert in the field; an unedited copy allows you freedom to find your own way.

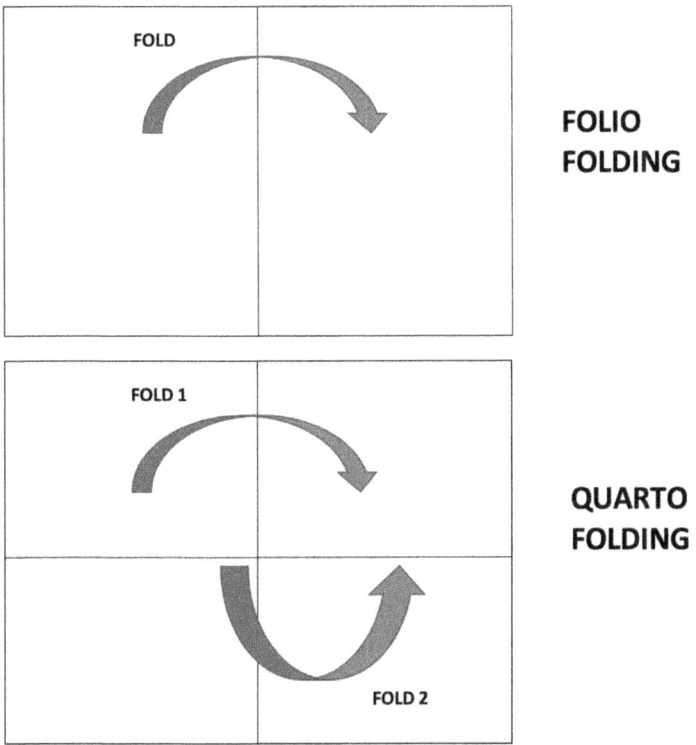

3.3 A single sheet of paper folded once (Folio) or twice (quarto) creates a range of different sizes.

Selecting a copy text

Copy texts can make a significant impact on your cut, so work from an edition you find trustworthy and useful to you. Each of our case studies are texts in the public domain, most of which are published in multiple forms. We always recommend you look through a few different editions before you settle on your copy text, as a nicely formatted copy might lack another edition's editorial content.

When you find your edition, take a moment to read through the editor's introduction, if it exists. Here, you may find useful insight into the history of the play in performance and publication. Discover:

1 Is this the only text available?
2 If not, are there differences between these several texts?
3 Does this difference matter? Regardless, which would I prefer to use?

42 *The Cutter's Toolkit Part One*

Let's lay out some hypotheticals here. Your group has planned Marlowe's *Dr. Faustus*, so you click on to Amazon (or, better, visit a local bookseller) and order the first copy at the top of the list (or the only one on the shelf). Great! Time to schedule rehearsal, right? Hold on. What do you have in your hands?

Antoni Cimolino:
The first thing we have to address is: anytime you pick up a copy of a play, you've got some *editor* (and I'm going to be careful since many of them are friends, right?) but they're trying to sell a book! Like: "new and improved!" which goes right back to the Folio: "Yes, well, this is the *real* version." And so after a while, you can only torture these texts—well, I suppose you can torture them infinitely—but sometimes you wonder: "Is that really a better word than the one that was in the Arden? Or in the last version of the Arden? Or in the one before that?" So you realize you can't just act like a beginner with Shakespeare who just picks up a play and that's the play. And then, of course, if you're doing *Lear* and you've got a Quarto with scenes that don't exist in the Folio, that are an entirely different thing in the Folio than in the Quarto, there's fundamental questions that come up with cutting. We're not talking about changing the text, but you're telling your own story, so you've got to get in there and you've got to make some cuts. The question you have to ask yourself is twofold: What story are you telling and why are you cutting?

3.4 Excerpt from interview with Antoni Cimolino, 12 February 2021.

We've deliberately chosen a volatile text. *Dr. Faustus* is an unstable script, published in two distinct documents well after Marlowe's violent and untimely death (the "A-Text" of 1604 and the "B-Text" of 1616). But what's the difference? It's pretty significant, actually. The B-Text is longer and differently structured, with additional scenes that do not appear in the A-Text, so this means they are materially two different plays. What's more, we have no sense of what this play contained in Marlowe's lifetime, but know it was profitable and popular enough to warrant publication 11 years after his death. We have little reason to believe every word corresponded to Marlowe's lost "foul papers." The B-Text (published 23 years after his death, nearly as long as Marlowe lived) is almost certainly the handiwork of embellishers who sought to pad the piece for one reason or another. So what edition do you use? What did your editor pick? Does your edition feature a mash-up of the two texts together? Do you go back to the A- or B-Texts or do you accept what your editor has included? Is it separate? Or conflated? It's worth knowing.

Here's another one. *The Glass Menagerie* (1945), which, being published relatively recently, is *not* legal to cut, exists in three iterations as a result of Tennessee Williams' tendency to edit after he published his editions.

The director must decide whether they will stage the 1945 *Reading* Edition, the 1948 *Acting* Edition, or the 1948 *London* Edition. Which one have you got? Which do you have the rights for? Have you read the other texts? Is there a reason for your choice, or do you trust the editor of your paperback to make the choice for you?

It is absolutely fine to trust the editor, if it will make this feel less daunting. However, if you want to dig around a little bit, you will not only find that you gain a much deeper sense of your play, but you might uncover some gold.

Start with what is important to you. Do you want a text which is clean and easy to read, or with the original punctuation? Do you care about the copy text? Are there variants?

Knowing your text

If you select an edited copy text, you might think, "No big deal, I'll trust the editor to pick my text for me." You *can*, but it's useful to know what's there. If you blindly follow the edited page, you may be deprived of insight. Similarly, to stick with a Folio-only text could deprive you of flourishes and details which might exist in other individually published texts. This adds a little time in the process, but can pay off in the end. *Romeo and Juliet*'s famous Chorus ("Two households, both alike in dignity...") doesn't appear in the First Folio. Were it not for the Q1 of 1597 and Q2 of 1599, we might not know this Chorus. Yet this speech appears in every *Romeo and Juliet* in every ninth-grade classroom ever. Even so, not every published edition of *Romeo and Juliet* uses the quartos as their copy-texts: rather, editors *choose to include* the Chorus speech, and will note this choice at the bottom of the page.

If you work from any academic edition, you'll notice the annotations at the bottom of each page. Some of these are explanatory, contextual notes, called the *gloss*. Editors use this useful section to explain references or allusions and offer historical context. This can be invaluable to help explain an obscure reference to an actor. Alongside the gloss, however, is a more mysterious section, which often seems like a secret code. These are the textual notes. For the casual reader, textual notes are easy to skip, but take a moment to look through it. This is a log of all editorial interventions on the page, which often includes historical choices made long ago and adopted by others. This section not only illustrates the choices the editor has made, but also shows the alternatives the editor *did not take*.

A textual note line from *Hamlet* might appear as follows:

496. *So, proceed you*] Q, omitted F.   502. match'd] Q, match F.
505. Then senseless Ilium] F, omitted Q.   506. this] Q, his F.   512. And like] F, Like Q.

3.5 Textual notes from *Hamlet*, the Arden Shakespeare, ed. Edward Dowden, 1899.

3.6 Variance notes can take many forms, including the inline presentation of the Internet Shakespeare Editions (left) and the list-based notes of the Folger Shakespeare (right).

We see from an indication of the numbered lines (496, 502, 505, 506, 512), the editor, Edward Dowden, has included a line ("So, proceed you") from Q (a quarto edition, which in this case refers to what is best known as Q2). Further, this notes variance from an alternate text (in this case, F) where "So proceed you" does not appear. So, the editor has chosen to incorporate this Q line omitted from F. We then see a reversal of this at line 505, where F's "Then senseless Ilium" does not appear in Q.

We also see variants: at line 502 Dowden prefers Q's "match'd" to F's "match"; at 506 he selects Q's "this" over F's "his"; and at 512, chooses F's "And like" to Q's "Like." These might seem like tiny details, but they're important. They show an editor has considered variance, and chose the best word from multiple editions. Someone else has done the work for you, which means you can avoid a dive into 400-year-old facsimiles to compare quartos and Folios (unless, of course, you really want to). If your edition asks Hamlet to say "oh, that this too, too sullied flesh…" but you prefer the F "solid" in place of the Q2 "sullied," you can make the change. If you are aware of your copy text, what your edition is based on, and what has come before, you know the options at your disposal. Keep in mind that this example is sourced from quite an old edited edition. If you are using an older edition, be aware that the scholarship might have expanded in more recent editions.

If you are using an online edition, investigate whether variance is noted: the Internet Shakespeare Editions have a toggle option to note uses of different texts, while the Folger Shakespeare features a separate page to list these changes. Take a look to see what is available: it may prove instructive.

Finally, and not insignificantly, remember that an edited edition is often collated for the distinct purpose of academic study, not performance. If an editor chooses a line reading that you disagree with, and you find an alternate line in the textual notes, you may choose to make a change.

Editors often also add stage directions for the benefit of readers. These are conventionally marked with square brackets. Take the "[*Aside*]" in this scene from Hannah Cowley's *A Bold Stroke for a Husband*:

VASQUEZ: Yes, so it is; but happily their distress is of that nature, that it generally goes off in a simper. But come, I'll send Marcella to you, and she will—
CAESAR: No, no; stay, my good friend. [*Gasping.*] You are in a violent hurry!
VASQUEZ: Why, truly, signor, at our time of life, when we determine to marry, we have no time to lose.
CAESAR: Why, that's very true, and so—oh! [*Aside*] St. Antony, now it comes to the point—but there can be no harm in looking at her—a look won't bind us for better or worse. Well, then, if you have a mind, I say, you may let me see her.

The editor, not Cowley, felt this line should be an aside. Imagine how Caesar's character would change if his ambivalence is *shared* with Vasquez instead of a private thought for the audience's ears alone.

If you take the textual notes into account, it will become quickly apparent that most published editions are *conflations*, which means the best elements from multiple sources are brought together to build a single text. It is up to us to unravel what the play is actually made up of before we can build on it. You educate yourself on the bibliographical history of your play. If it exists in multiple forms, be aware of it, even if you set this information aside. Scholarship over the last generation has advocated for the de-conflation of multiple texts, where each published text can be judged on its own merits. If your edition was edited in the 1980s, it's likely your scholarship is not up to date. A dusty edition from the middle of the last century or sourced online might be handy, but the scholarship has probably expired. If you can find an academic edition published in the last decade, you will benefit from the fruits of all this labor.

As for textual variance? Ultimately, it's immaterial to everyday life in the rehearsal hall. If your edition is a quarto-based cut but you find a line or option you like from the Folio, then by all means use it. Some scholars (present company included) fixate on textual variance between editions, but remember: you want to create a practical text, not a historiographical conundrum.

Line numbers

Line numbers might well change from text to text. Line numbers are usually applied by editors to guide their annotations, so the reader knows exactly where to apply the note and not interrupt their flow. Some editions add asterisks or other flags to alert the reader there is a note at the bottom of the page, but this can be disruptive. In any case, line numbers (and what's more, scene and act numbers) are *often* a modern editorial addition. We are very familiar with the neoclassical ideal of the five-act structure, but few plays from the early modern era are published with indicated act and scene numbers. Most of those were applied by later editors, and adopted by their successors. Again, there's nothing wrong with this: it's handy to say to your actors, "Today we'll run Act Two, Scene Four," and for everyone to know what that means. What you can't do, however, is ask everyone to provide their own paperback edition and assume line, scene, and act numbers always match. Toby ran across this issue early in his career as an actor in *Macbeth*, where every performer had their own haphazardly selected paperback, and the inconsistent presence of the "Hecate scene" played havoc with scene numbering.

You may want to maintain line numbers in your edition, for ease of communication in rehearsal. Saying, "Michael, on line 22, think about a downward inflection," is quick and easy. Ensure that lineation is standard throughout your edition. You can add numbers manually or follow what's in your copy text. A standard in editorial circles is the Through Line Numbering (TLN) system, applied by scholar Charlton Hinman to his 1968 Norton Facsimile edition of Shakespeare's F1. TLN numbers lines consistently through the play, rather than restarting line counts in each scene. So, in *Hamlet*, "Who's there?" is line 4 (after stage directions), and "Go, bid the soldiers shoot" is line 3904. This means with universal line numbering, we can say to any scholar, "I live my life by the adage in line 543 of the F1 *Hamlet*," and they can easily find the reference. Prior to TLN, you risked confusion if you glibly tossed out a line number.

TLNs are rarely used in modern published editions: most will reset line numbers at the beginning of the next scene, but it's a useful tool if you have the patience to add it, particularly if you've made cuts and need to re-line your edition. You might find your stage manager plans to number the lines regardless in their prompt book—an entirely personal preference: some re-number every line even if you've supplied them—but in our experience line numbers ensure the entire production is on the same page, so to speak.

The physical (or digital?) script

Once you've made your decisions on editions or texts, take a moment to consider *presentation*. How will you provide your cast and production team with scripts? If you've gone the edited edition route, do you mass-order a carton of books from Penguin or Doubleday and apply textual changes in tablework? Do you make a single master copy and print, scan, or photocopy it? Do you type it up with cuts excised, or leave the cut lines visible in case there are changes in rehearsal? Everyone in your company must work from an identical copy of the script. This means when someone refers to "Scene Three," or "line 201," or "page 19," you all go to the same place. It also means everyone has exactly the same words on the page. If actors have to cross-reference what their edition says, that can be a major time waster in rehearsal.

If you choose to use a published edition, there are obvious benefits. The paperback format means actors don't fuss with loose sheets of paper. They usually come with handy contextual introductions and annotations. Your stage manager might be forced to cut their edition up to create a prompt-book, but that's to be expected. If you go this route, though, not only do you need to take into account the *content* of a published edition, but also its *presentation*.

For example, academic publishers, such as Routledge, Cambridge, Oxford, and Bloomsbury offer a brilliant range of in-depth analytical play texts. Editors often design these for the classroom and the scholar, and feature insightful notes on the minutiae of the world of the play and playwright. This can be useful in the rehearsal room when the cast works to analyze the text, but the sheer quantity of gloss and textual notes can often interrupt the reader's flow. Sometimes a lengthy contextual note means only a line or two of dialog makes it to the page. This is no problem whatsoever to the scholar, but actors might prefer a text which minimizes page-turns. Scholarly editions are most useful for dramaturgical context on the fly, but if you can, provide the company an actor-friendly edition with space for notes and a font large enough easily read.

Of course, if you provide a published edition as your copy text, you will need to take into account how you will present cut lines: we discuss this in greater depth in later chapters.

Weapon of choice

All of the materials we have described are useful and accessible. They were mentioned often in our interview process. These are tools we have come to rely on, often as a result of trial and error or simple necessity. Compiling all of these materials might result in redundancy and double-handling—for example, don't fret about spreadsheets if it makes more sense to write things out—so we urge you to be selective in your approach. Try a few ways to see what works for you.

At the same time, we do not pretend this approach to materials is exhaustive; if you have materials which work for you, apply them alongside our tips.

With physical materials in hand, let's put them to good use with strategies and considerations you might want to bring on board when you shape your text.

Works cited

Hinman, Charlton, ed. *The First Folio of Shakespeare*. New York: Paul Hamlyn, 1968.

Malone, Toby. "Parallel-text Analysis and Practical Dramaturgies." *Routledge Companion to Dramaturgy*. London: Routledge, 2015. https://doi.org/10.4324/9780203075944

Neville, Sarah. "1. Editing English Renaissance Texts". *Handbook of English Renaissance Literature*, edited by Ingo Berensmeyer, Berlin, Boston: De Gruyter, 2019, pp. 27–45. https://doi.org/10.1515/9783110444889-002

4 The Cutter's Toolkit Part Two

Strategies and Considerations

You have your tools. You have your director's concept. You know your space and cast limitations and expected line count. You have started to trim and snip and winnow, maybe hesitatingly, maybe with a chainsaw. But what happens in those inevitable moments when it becomes impossible to see the forest for the trees? There will be days when the task of removing hundreds of lines daunts all the more as you agonize over a single word. Often, strategies and considerations—tricks of the trade—will help you get unstuck. Many of these elements, learned through trial and error, offer perspectives on cut processes to help guide you through these difficult times. Often, bold decisions around a specific approach will set you on a positive course.

Liposuction vs amputation

You can cut a lot from a play with big, slashing blows to remove entire scenes, characters, or subplots. However, liposuction is preferable to amputation, although both approaches can be part of your cutter's toolkit. For an audience with some familiarity with your subject, you can get away with more when you trim the text by a little bit from lots of places than by removal of big chunks. You're also less likely to do unexpected damage to the structure.

As we have said, plays are constructed for a reason. Playwrights include lines, scenes, and characters to propel a narrative and explore a world. For a play to survive, it must have been successful enough in one of its early forms to be repeated, then recorded, and distributed. You make no claim to know more than the playwright when you dare to cut their play: you simply adapt your given material based on the parameters you set.

These parameters inform what gets to stay and what has to go. Every cut is different, which is why amputation (large-scale cuts) or liposuction (subtle, granular cuts) may be right for you. But how do you know what *is* right for you? To turn back to a handy example from Shakespeare, we can consider the impact of "amputation" on the narrative as a whole.

Take the "Queen Mab" speech, from *Romeo and Juliet*. At first glance, it feels superfluous (purists, bear with us!). It doesn't advance the plot much, and doesn't have a great deal to do with the overall story. Maybe it's shoved

DOI: 10.4324/9781003160076-5

Antoni Cimolino:
You know you gotta make some choices: do you make elegant little internal cuts and preserve these themes? I remember [actor] Douglas Rain saying: never allow a director to cut your first words in a Shakespeare play, because Shakespeare is telling the audience who you are. And he knows what he's doing. He's a craftsperson. He knows that he's introducing a character on that stage in subtle ways. It's not going to be direct. He is going to begin to put spin on the ball and let the audience know who you are and if you mess with those words, it has a bigger price than if you mess with something later on.

4.1 Excerpt from interview with Antoni Cimolino, 12 February 2021.

in to give the actor who plays Mercutio a chance to show off or to allow time for another actor to change costumes. These 40 or so lines take a competent actor a solid ten minutes, an indulgent one, longer. Why not remove it, whole cloth?

Three key reasons:

1   You don't want to have *that* argument with the actor playing Mercutio.
2   Your audience will notice. Unless you have a good artistic reason for it, you're better off not to remove lines everyone knows, because they will ask where they've gone. Few will notice if you eliminate whole scenes of "Lord Capulet, Wedding Planner," but cut Queen Mab at your peril.
3   It turns out your actor was right: This speech is important, and not just because it makes him look good. Mercutio has relatively little stage time. Without Queen Mab, he doesn't have a chance to connect with the audience and make himself a real, important person in their eyes. If his death doesn't matter to them, Romeo's reaction to it—and therefore, the rest of the play—doesn't make sense.

An amputation cut of Queen Mab slams the play right after Juliet learns of Paris's suit into the Montague boys' arrival at the party, with little transition, context, or banter. Mercutio's witty nonsense might *look* cuttable, but examine what this amputation does to the rest of the body. Consider liposuction. Do we really need every detail of her carriage? Can we take out a few of her pranks? As long as you retain "O, then, I see Queen Mab hath been with you," you can remove half of this speech and the vast majority will never notice, but you still give the actor enough time to become memorable and important to them.

"Liposuction" can take many forms. While wholesale excision is a uniform change, a liposuction cut can be tailored to the production or to the director's

Antoni Cimolino:
[Director] Nicholas Pennell would turn a script on its side, and look for "skyscrapers and apartment buildings." The big long speeches would be a big long apartment building, whereas a rapid exchange between two characters would be a series of skyscrapers. So you're changing the landscape literally as you decide what goes and what stays. Even doing things like cutting spectacle, fights, dances, cutting the gods arriving on an eagle's back, you're again changing the rhythm of the play. Because in Shakespeare, every 20 minutes there's something fun. So you can say, well, I'm not gonna cut the words, I'll cut the other 'stuff' but the fight at that point in *Romeo and Juliet* is every bit as important as the words: not just for plot, but also for the feeling of the evening where he's trying to get you to a certain point.

4.2 Excerpt from interview with Antoni Cimolino, 12 February 2021.

vision. It can call out elements of the production or avoid tongue-twister words the actor struggles with. Here are Toby's and Aili's production cuts of the "Queen Mab" speech. Aili's cuts are italicized, Toby's are in bold. Notice where we overlap and where we differ. Aili's cut is more aggressive because she had a tighter time constraint for the overall production. Both versions of the speech were well-received by audiences: nobody wondered where their favorite line had gone.

> O, then I see Queen Mab hath been with you.
> She is the fairies' midwife, and she comes
> In shape no bigger than an agate stone
> On the forefinger of an alderman,
> Drawn with a team of little atomi
> Over men's noses as they lie asleep.
> *Her wagon spokes made of long spinners' legs,*
> *The cover of the wings of grasshoppers,*
> **Her traces of the smallest spider web,**
> **Her collars of the moonshine's wat'ry beams,**
> *Her whip of cricket's bone, the lash of film,*
> *Her wagoner a small gray-coated gnat,*
> *Not half so big as a round little worm*
> *Pricked from the lazy finger of a maid.*
> *Her chariot is an empty hazelnut,*
> *Made by the joiner squirrel or old grub,*
> *Time out o' mind the fairies' coachmakers.*
> And in this state she gallops night by night

Through lovers' brains, and then they dream of love;
On courtiers' knees, that dream on cur'sies straight;
O'er lawyers' fingers, who straight dream on fees;
O'er ladies' lips, who straight on kisses dream,
Which oft the angry Mab with blisters plagues
Because their breaths with sweetmeats tainted are.
Sometime she gallops o'er a courtier's nose,
And then dreams he of smelling out a suit.
And sometime comes she with a tithe-pig's tail,
Tickling a parson's nose as he lies asleep;
Then he dreams of another benefice.
Sometime she driveth o'er a soldier's neck,
And then dreams he of cutting foreign throats,
Of breaches, ambuscadoes, Spanish blades,
Of healths five fathom deep, and then anon
Drums in his ear, at which he starts and wakes
And, being thus frighted, swears a prayer or two
And sleeps again. This is that very Mab
That plats the manes of horses in the night
And bakes the elflocks in foul sluttish hairs,
Which once untangled much misfortune bodes.
This is the hag, when maids lie on their backs,
That presses them and learns them first to bear,
Making them women of good carriage.
This is she.

How much is too much?

Say, for example, you are tasked with a cut of *Macbeth*. Your company requires a one-hour production, and you have access to eight actors. They'd really like you to focus on Lady Macbeth's story overall. You shred the witches' scenes back to their main narrative functions, remove battlefield reports, thin many of the speeches, and remove (sorry!) the Porter's shenanigans. Donalbain's gone, merged with his brother. Out with Seyton and young Siward. Ross and the Old Man are essentially only present at the banquet. Banquo and Fleance are stripped back to a brief glimpse prior to the attack, Hecate is (obviously) toast, Lady Macduff and her pretty chickens die offstage, Malcolm accepts Macduff's help but doesn't test him, and the sleepwalk becomes a sleepstroll. Battles are shorn to the quick, the title character's introspection is brief, and his death is nasty, brutish, and short. This is an extreme cut. Arguably, not a very good one, either. But is it still *Macbeth*? When does it stop being so? It retains many of Shakespeare's words, characters, and scenarios, but it's almost nothing like the play Shakespeare wrote. Can we still call it Shakespeare's *Macbeth*?
   Yes.

Removing text does not deauthorize a play, since text is only one pillar on which a play is built, alongside character and narrative. If this structural tripod has one of its legs undermined or removed, it unbalances the production. If we set such judgement aside for a moment, a play with the words removed but which retains characters and narratives is still worthwhile. If not, then how could we classify translations as part of an author's canon? François-Victor Hugo's "Être, ou ne pas être, c'est là la question" does not use Shakespeare's words, but maintains its spirit and tone. *A Doll's House* played in American Sign Language remains Ibsen: it is just a different version of it. However, if you took *Macbeth*, changed the names of the characters, set the play in a fast-food restaurant, and updated the production design to 1970s kitsch, you verge far more into adaptation territory (we just described the criminally underrated film *Scotland, PA.*). American-Georgian experimental performance troupe Synetic famously performs a "wordless Shakespeare" (a phrase the company acknowledges as oxymoronic) which is thrillingly textual, as the words themselves are translated into physical movement. Do we disassociate Shakespeare's name from Tchaikovsky's *Romeo and Juliet* ballet? Or Verdi's *Otello*? Ultimately, there is more to a play than just the author's words. Linda Hutcheon told us that there is not a clear line:

> I've always felt that there was a kind of spectrum of adaptational practices, if you like: from what we usually think of as adapting (within one medium or across media) through exactly what you are talking about with cutting plays—and translations, for instance. It's hard to draw the line between the different practices—and why would one want to do that? Labels are just heuristic devices, right?

For the purposes of this book, however, we employ that heuristic device, focusing tightly on cutting. If you are curious about adaptation, we highly recommend Hutcheon's seminal work, *A Theory of Adaptation*.

Text cutting, itself a form of adaptation, is often a process of microsurgery, but sometimes it's a bloodbath. Cutting as much or as little of a play as is necessary to your production does not make it *not* Shakespeare. Or *not* Congreve. Or *not* Behn. It makes it a *version* of those works. There is no Plimsoll line on a play which tips it over to being no longer the author's play, any more than radical design interventions interfere with the author's ownership of a work. Cuts are historically standard in performance, to make a play fit a certain space, audience, or moment.

Rearrangement and relocation, or, not all cuts are cuts

While our discussion revolves primarily around the process of text cuts, you may occasionally find opportunities to make changes which are not a cut. Textual rearrangement is another tool in your dramaturgical kit worth consideration.

If you move sections of text or entire stories to a different location in the play, you cause fundamental changes to the play's structure. Plays are structured in their received chronological form for a purpose, with the notable exception of Georg Büchner's *Woyzeck,* posthumously published and discovered in fragments, rearranged, and presented in various chronologies. Sophie Treadwell places the first encounter between "The Young Woman" and "The Man" past the midpoint of *Machinal* for a good reason: the narrative builds to a point where his introduction can have a solid impact.

If you were to relocate this "story" to the start of the play, you would destabilize the text in many ways. Yet it might also add the possibility for the audience to anticipate what is to come, and remind them this edit is a new take on a familiar text. A text shift can foreground vital elements. In Toby's production of *King Lear,* he moved Edmund's "Gods stand up for bastards" speech to the first scene of the play (based, in part, on Nahum Tate's 1681 structure), even before the division of the kingdom. The audience had settled themselves in to see a play they felt they already knew, and this signaled change from the top, which put the group on notice that this was a different angle on a familiar work.

Rearrangement, of course, can't be taken lightly. You might choose to rearrange text to clarify a narrative moment, or to support a doubling choice. Sometimes, you can achieve this with little major impact, but other instances

4.3 Alex Hedly as the Young Woman in *Machinal* at Penn State Harrisburg, 2020.

require finesse. There is precedent for such rearrangement: the Q1 text of *Hamlet*, published in 1603, places Hamlet's "To be or not to be" speech (with unfamiliar wording, no less) at an earlier point in the play than what we might expect. In Q1, Hamlet speaks "To be or not to be" in Act Two, Scene Two, or at the point at which Hamlet "enters, reading on a book." Compared to Q2/F, this brings his confrontation with Ophelia forward by a full act, before the entrance of the Players. In Q2 and F, the "To be" speech appears in Act Three, Scene One, in between Hamlet's scenes with the Players. This story rearrangement demonstrates how a section can be lifted out and relocated, which refocuses narrative and emphasis. While the "To be or not to be" speech is importantly positioned in Act Three, its relocation can signal an artistic choice to keep the audience on their toes. This speech, so iconic as to be a given in any version of the play, is self-contained enough to bear relocation, and indeed it is not uncommon to see modern producers shift the speech back to Act Two.

Rearranged speeches and entire scenes can disrupt the narrative flow, but this can be beneficial. Ultimately, the text cutter must be as aware as possible that many audience members might have watched this play performed multiple different times over the course of their lives, until they could recite along with the actors. There's nothing wrong with the play exactly as-is, in the conventional structure. Yet we have found great benefit in subverted expectations.

Another useful structural innovation is to merge scenes together, in an "interleaved" style which can highlight similarities in theme or structure. This allows the audience to effectively see two scenes at once, juxtaposed in real time. Martine Kei Green-Rogers spoke of an Oregon Shakespeare Festival *Romeo and Juliet*, directed by Bill Rauch, which interleaved the scene in which the Nurse tells Juliet that Romeo has killed Tybalt, with the scene where Romeo and the Friar process the same event. These scenes played at the same time, and highlighted their parallels for the audience.

Do you ever rearrange stuff?
James Evans:
With our most recent *Dream*, we started with the Mechanicals. We went straight into "Is all our company here?" …We started with Bottom wanting to play all the parts. In our production the Mechanicals were also playing all the lovers. So we cut from "Enough. Hold or cut bowstrings." We lost "Hold or cut bowstrings." Bottom just said, "Enough!" and then we had a big scene change. Puck came in and swept everything off the tables, and everyone put on these "court" coats, and sat down, and suddenly there were Theseus and Egeus and Hermia and Lysander, and we started that scene.

4.4 Excerpt from interview with James Evans, 1 February 2021.

Interleaved scenes can also help spice up a scene necessary for the plot, but laborious to perform. Tim Carroll shared his solution for this problem in *Macbeth*, where Act Four, Scene Three fills in a lot of the plot, but "is an area of quicksand that most productions drown in." He interleaved this scene with Act Four, Scene One, where Macbeth visits the witches for the last time. "I was trying to give the turning point a double force," he told us.

> Macbeth heard good news about Birnam Wood and Dunsinane, and 'No man of woman born.' He heard better and better news. Macduff heard worse and worse news about how evil Malcolm was, and then at the same moment, Malcolm said, 'I was only testing you,' and the witches say, 'You won't give birth to a line of kings.'

The clearer story of the witches' prophetic peripeteia provided a scaffold for the more political and obscure reversal Malcolm offers. Another *Macbeth* at the Stratford Festival, Canada merged Malcolm and Macduff's scene with the murder of Macduff's family, creating a chilling tone as Macduff learned the news simultaneous to (for the audience) the assault itself.

Obviously, rearrangement should make narrative sense: as we've suggested, narrative is one of the three legs of the structural tripod to support a play. *The Seagull* beginning with Konstantin's attempted suicide requires a great deal of additional work to draw the piece back from the edge of abstraction and the avant-garde. Unless, of course, such fragmentation is by design, in the tradition of artists such as Charles Marowitz.

Rearrangement and relocation restructure the narrative of the play, which means they should be undertaken with caution. Scenes which rely on the content of the previous scene for narrative sense are difficult to rearrange, but often a judicious cut can compact narrative expediently enough to avoid a scene break altogether. As you think about structure, consider what rearrangement might do. Such elements are akin to cuts: they alter the overall fabric of the piece.

Patching the holes

As you cut, you might wish for a quick, simple way to carry the audience with you across a gap in the story. Many of the experts we spoke with described adopting lines from other plays by the same playwright. This allowed them to maintain the sound and feel of the text. Audience members never noticed. If you feel especially brave (and familiar with your playwright), you might even add a few lines of your own. Tina Packer shared that her mentor, John Barton, did this frequently.

> He was the only person I know who would add lines of Shakespeare. And there were a few occasions when I cut, I thought, 'Oh that doesn't really make sense, but I'm not going to put it back in because we're on

a time constraint. I'm going to write a line of Shakespeare so it makes sense.' John Barton used to do it all the time, so I kind of feel I have permission to do it.

Kate Mulvany took it a step further, and used Shakespeare's source material to bridge a big chunk of action. "The last third of *Julius Caesar* really is the battle ground. All of these extra characters get brought in, but who cares?" she told us.

> They've been lost to history. For that adaptation, I took dead Portia and gave her Plutarch's beautiful account of what happened on the battlefield. It's very haunting and very poetic. He says very clearly which side the battalions were coming from. It's a really clear idea of the war that they were in. To have Portia's ghost telling the audience, that was like a Greek chorus way of telling the audience what happened, without having to stage a full war.

It's a creative solution to one of the core problems of the play. The audience will notice these kinds of additions, of course. One audience member, who knew that Mulvany, onstage as Cassius, had adapted the text, stood up and yelled at her for this choice *in the middle of a performance*. Still: if you have an idea this brilliant, don't let potential pedantic audience members stop you.

Doubling

Here's another tricky one: you have a cast of eight actors to perform a play with more roles than bodies. You need to make some kind of adjustment, which comes down to two alternatives: either cut or double. It is not usually the cutter's sole decision to double characters; check with your organization in case they had hoped an apprentice actor would play the Theban messenger before you slash them out. Otherwise, you may need to consider doubling your assets.

Doubling refers to the decision to have one actor play more than one role, often with a costume change, with little internal acknowledgement of the change. This has been a common practice throughout world theatre history, as it is now, for an unchanging reason: efficiency. You don't want to pay union scale for somebody to hang around in the greenroom all night, only to come onstage for 40 seconds and say, "I will, my lord."

While doubling doesn't necessarily require editing, judicious cuts can help solve some challenges. Sometimes, a doubling chart falls apart because there's *one scene* where two characters who could otherwise be played by the same actor are onstage together. Cutting asks, "But do they *have to*?" Cuts allow you to open opportunities to look at bumps in an otherwise smooth doubling chart and consider whether those lines are absolutely necessary, or might be logically assigned to another character.

The obvious risk for doubling is to ensure characters can be played by the one actor without major logistical challenges, such as if they are on stage in the same scene, or in back-to-back scenes. It also brings up logical concerns: to cast the same actor as soldiers on opposite sides of a war asks more of the audience than a simple blind eye. If you have these considerations in hand, you can double to bring your cast to a manageable level.

Intermissions

Most productions which run over 90 minutes include a break for the audience to stretch, use the restroom, and get a drink. In many modern plays, an often non-negotiable intermission or act break is included by the playwright. Not so with classical works. Placement of the intermission can be an afterthought, but it has a massive impact on the experience for the audience and actors alike. Amidst a disagreement on the placement of an act break in Shakespeare, Toby once suggested an artistic director consider a cut without an intermission. The response? The tour company depended on the concession stand income at intermission, so a break was vital. Sodas over structure.

As you cut, try to keep in mind where you'll put the intermission; generally, it's better to have the segment prior to the break be a bit longer than the one afterward. The intermission is a signal to the audience that your performance is at least halfway over. If you have 45 minutes before the intermission, but 90 after, you'll notice your audience grow antsy midway through the second act.

Many plays in the public domain come from theatrical traditions with different expectations about intermissions than modern audiences. Lue Douthit was quick to point out the ways an intermission disrupts the intended structure of the play: "You are throwing a huge wrench into an already whole thing that never was there. So you are arbitrarily trying to make it fit our cookie cutter." Plays originally performed in open-air spaces, from *The Libation Bearers* (5th century BCE) to *Life is a Dream* (1635), generally did not have an intermission. A break in the action would give the audience a chance to lose interest and wander off, not to mention waste precious sunlight hours. Plays written for pre-electric indoor spaces often required regular breaks to trim and relight the candles. If you insert an intermission in the middle of *Every Man in His Humour* (1598), you add a break it never had, while if you bifurcate *The Knight of the Burning Pestle* (1607), you ignore the fact that it was probably divided into five parts.

With this said, an audience will usually expect an intermission, so where you place it matters. In our many conversations with experts, all voiced despair at intermission placement. Do you break when the suspense builds to a crucial moment, so people return eager for the next piece of the action, or right after it, and leave the audience thrilled and hungry for more?

Some of the more intriguing—and daring—intermission placements are those which break in the middle of a scene, rather than at an act or scene break.

Tim Carroll shared an intermission idea for *Julius Caesar* which was left, so to speak, on the cutting room floor: "I wanted the interval to be right after 'Tyranny is dead.' You'd come back up for the second half at the same moment, one second later." We would have liked to see that—a cut which would allow the energy and power of the most famous section of *Caesar* to draw people back after intermission and get the second half off to an energetic start.

Lue Douthit chuckled with glee over one *Romeo and Juliet* intermission placement. "We split the 'gallop apace' speech in half," she explained.

> That's where we put the intermission. I always send people to listen in the line at the ladies' room because that's where you're going to get all the good information about how people are receiving the play, and yes, point in fact, everyone was like, 'I can't believe they cut that speech!' and I just thought, 'Ha ha ha, wait til the top of the second act. It's coming back.'

Douthit's team used the familiarity of "Gallop apace" as a hook to help audience members focus back into the world of the play after the break. One production of *Hamlet* we saw at the Stratford Festival placed the intermission right in the middle of Hamlet's "Now I might do it pat" speech, with his sword raised inexorably over the unaware Claudius, only to return from intermission with the "cliffhanger" resolved: Hamlet has second thoughts and Claudius is temporarily spared, as if there were any doubt.

Wherever you place your intermission, whether you decide on a traditional placement or an avant garde one, don't leave it until the last minute. It's an important decision, and it affects the structure of the whole piece.

What's in a word?

One consideration which emerges is word *replacement*: to rephrase text to ensure audience comprehension. Why not remove a difficult or offensive word and replace it with a safer, simpler one? Sometimes, this is a good strategy, particularly for a specific audience, to simplify a potentially uncomfortable moment in terms of word choice. This can be an easy decision, as some casual early modern racism (with references to skin color or religion) hit the ear of a modern audience in a particularly striking manner. Of course, this is part of the point: to cut or rewrite classical texts to smooth out the rough edges smacks of the well-meant but misguided moralistic work of Thomas Bowdler, who rewrote Shakespeare in the 19th century to remove content he felt did not represent family values.

As with all potential cuts or changes, you must carefully consider any word replacement for its ultimate result. We once saw a conservative high school production of *A Midsummer Night's Dream* "cleaned up" so thoroughly that the young actors were not allowed to say Bottom had transformed into an "ass," regardless of the definition of the word.

James Shapiro:
I would say that as somebody's cutting the text that we do not change the words. Once in a while, I will come up against an experienced director who will say, "I don't like that word, audiences won't know what it means, change it." My feeling is that in 99% of circumstances a good actor can convey what that word means. So I fiercely resist it. But the director's the director, it's their show, but I always put up a fight. I do not want to change the language of Shakespeare, I think that's dangerous.

4.5 Excerpt from interview with James Shapiro, 8 February 2021.

Sometimes word choice is crucial: James Shapiro talked of his work on Alfredo Michel Modenessi's 2021 bilingual Spanish-English *Romeo Y Julieta*. Shapiro recounted a note he offered on a line which translated Juliet's "thy lips are warm" into Spanish, with an extended syllable count which undercut the moment. The translator agreed and restored the English original. Antoni Cimolino recalled Robert LePage's Québécois translation of *Coriolanus*, where the translation of the definitive line "thou hast done a deed that would make valor weep" excised the concept of "valor:" a major shift in the moment. Lue Douthit noted the power of individual words, such as the repetition of the word "authority" in *Troilus and Cressida*. In that play, the actor playing Hector fought for a restored cut after he realized he was the last character to use the word "honor." "The minute he leaves the stage," Douthit told us, "honor leaves the stage." In both instances, these words had major importance; we should be careful when we cut them.

One easy method to spot important words is to create "word clouds" of the text—either the whole play, an act, a scene, or a character's lines. Increased text size is based on the number of occurrences of the word, so these visualizations draw your attention to keywords you might have missed. For example, in these word clouds of the two texts of *Dr. Faustus* (please see Figures 4.6 and 4.7), notice how "hell," "soul," "God," "Lucifer," "now," and "come" jump out at you in the A-text. Cut them with care. This comparison also allows you to quickly see many key differences between the two texts. Making word clouds can be a hassle—we have tools for them at www.cuttingplays.com.

Text changes are a tool to maintain in your toolkit: you are not legally prevented from it, even if many directors and text editors resist the temptation. Specific word choices are deliberate and have stood the test of time, so change text with care. A strong actor will glean sense from an

4.6 A-text of Dr. Faustus

obtuse phrase to make it clear to the audience. In his 2013 film adaptation of *Romeo and Juliet*, Julian Fellowes liberally changed heightened language for the benefit of the audience, as he believed that ordinary audiences, lacking his Cambridge education, would struggle to understand the text. His choices (demonstrated in the Nurse's over-simplified complaints about her back) distracted and ironically alienated in different ways, summarized in critical scorn (see Figure 4.8).

We try to stick with the words the playwright gave us, unless they are entirely untenable (or if you happen to be John Barton). If it's verse, you should try to match the rhythm, and at the very least it should be a change which will not call attention to itself. Ultimately, we've found, it's exceedingly rare to come up with a word better than the one the playwright chose. Tweak with caution.

The Cutter's Toolkit Part Two 61

4.7 B-text of Dr. Faustus

Common ground

One thing all cuts have in common is this: they take time. It's rare to develop a good, complete, rehearsal-ready cut in a single session. You might need to schedule a read-through to hear how it sounds (or speak it aloud to yourself!). If you're able, engage a couple of friends or company members to sit in as an audience to listen to the cut. Try to match this test audience to a real one. Take special note of tricky spots or especially audacious choices. Listen hard for sense, flow, and overall scene logic. Keep time: is your cut too long or not long enough? Always remember, though: actorly business will take up more time, and actorly familiarity with the script will tighten it back up.

As you listen for your "question mark" spots, try not to telegraph their presence among your listeners—"Listen to this speech. Tell me if it sounds weird to you," is a surefire way to make it sound weird—but allow it to flow

	F1 (1623)		Julian Fellowes (2013)
NURSE	Lord, how my head aches, what a head have I!	**NURSE**	How my head aches, what a head I have!
	It beats as it would fall in twenty pieces.		It throbs as it would break in twenty bits!
	My back, a 'tother side, O, my back, my back!		And my back - my back is killing me!
	Beshrew your heart for sending me about		It's all your fault for sending me to town!
	To catch my death with jaunting up and down.		

4.8 Julian Fellowes made some distinctive choices in attempting to make his 2013 *Romeo and Juliet* text more accessible.

to see if it works. Sometimes you need to hear it to know you've cut too much. Once you've heard all your "question mark" spots, take a casual poll to see whether they stood out as problematic to your listener. Did they work for you? How was it for the actors who had to speak those words? If anyone's confused, now's the time to unravel why. If you've cut too much and you've just now realized the third messenger actually *was* important, you can always adjust your cut. You can add most cuts back in, if we assume you have the time and a plan for who will say the words, but if you're in tech week, that's a recipe for trouble.

After you've finished, have a casual conversation with the listeners and actors. What did they like? What stood out? What did they miss? Unless you've made a *huge* choice ("Doesn't Oedipus usually self-harm in some way? What happened there?"), chances are no one noticed. If it's a play they're familiar with, they might, which is fine. An actor who leads with, "Wow, I saw you put 'To be or not to be' in the last act," doesn't necessarily think it's wrong (it's certainly bold). A cut can be whatever you need it to be. It can be bold, but it can also be safe. The point of this process is to find out whether it works. Does it tell the story? Are the characters still clear? Will the audience receive the information? Will anyone notice? In a very rare turn of events, *Toronto Star* critic Robert Crew noted a *Midsummer Night's Dream* cut Toby staged had been "trimmed, but not butchered." The text had actually been reduced by nearly 30%. It remains a source of pride that what this knowledgeable critic saw as a mere "trim" was much more extensive.

Sometimes the best cuts are the cuts no one notices.

Turn to Appendix 2 for activities to try your hand at the process. Many of these tools and tips should provide sufficient insight to set you on your way.

Works cited

Crew, Robert. "Theatre in the Park Worth Seeing." *The Toronto Star.* 4 July 2007. https://www.thestar.com/entertainment/stage/2007/07/04/theatre_in_the_park_worth_seeing.html

Hutcheon, Linda. *A Theory of Adaptation: Second Edition.* New York: Routledge, 2013.

Marowitz, Charles. *The Marowitz Shakespeare: Adaptions* (sic) *and Collages of Hamlet, MacBeth, the Taming of the Shrew, Measure for Measure, and the Merchant of Venice.* London: Drama Publishers, 1979.

5 Cut to the Quick
Character-Specific Cuts

Playwrights fill the worlds of their plays with characters who interact, drive narrative forward, and create conflict to produce drama. In this chapter, we consider the logistics of character-specific cuts. Sometimes, the quickest way to take 15 minutes from a play is to remove a character entirely, or merge two or more together, and cut redundant lines. Cuts can target a specific character to trim them back to a minor supporting role, or can change how the audience understands their personality, motivation, and choices.

Cutting by character may seem an easy way to reduce your cast size and line count, but it's obviously not quite so simple. Characters are invariably intertwined, in conversation and interaction, and removing one can often leave a serious gap. A production of *Miss Julie* without Christine is certainly a lot shorter, but it also means the information Christine brings is either lost or must be redistributed. Even if you were to accept the loss of this content, taking out Christine entirely undercuts the dramatic tension of Julie and Jean's relationship. Here, a major character cut impacts the structure of the work, so must be undertaken carefully.

Featured or minimized characters

Productions frequently cut to specifically feature a particular character.

A cutter might take *Hedda Gabler* (1891) and instinctively cut other characters' lines more frequently than the title character's. It *is* Hedda's play, after all. Doing this *on purpose* is an excellent frame for a production. Doing it by accident is lazy. We encourage cuts which come from choices, not assumptions. An equally good *Hedda Gabler* cut could *minimize* Hedda's lines to focus on her impact on others and the way the household orbits around her: an ensemble piece rather than a star vehicle.

In this example, Miss Tesman pays a call on her nephew Tesman and his new bride, Hedda. We've cut it first to feature Hedda. Notice how the other characters have less space to develop a personal connection with the audience; Hedda holds the spotlight.

DOI: 10.4324/9781003160076-6

On Queen Margaret, *a conflation of the* Henry VI *plays and* Richard III:
Megan McDonough:
What's interesting in cutting toward a character: the first thing you do is pull every scene the character's in, and every time the character's talked about, and those moments become sacrosanct: you feel like you can't cut any mention of her specifically, you can't cut any of her lines; I would say cutting in general, even beyond Margaret, I am very careful when cutting womens' lines because they're already at a disadvantage and I don't want to see that. I focus on cutting the windbag main character lines to make the parts seem more even. So if I'm cutting a scene between two characters and one is Margaret, I'm going to cut more of the other character to make Margaret the star of the show. With *Margaret* I found a lot of ways of cutting mentions of her from other scenes into things so I wasn't just taking giant chunks, but intricately putting stuff together. I never had to lose a great line of hers or a great mention of her. I could slip it in to make it make sense.

5.1 Excerpt from interview with Megan McDonough, 9 February 2021.

MISS TESMAN: Good morning, my dear Hedda! Good morning, and a hearty welcome!
HEDDA: Good morning, dear Miss Tesman! So early a call! That is kind of you.
MISS TESMAN: Well—has the bride slept well in her new home?
HEDDA: Oh yes, thanks. Passably.
TESMAN: Passably! Come, that's good, Hedda! You were sleeping like a stone when I got up.
HEDDA: Fortunately. Of course one has always to accustom one's self to new surroundings, Miss Tesman—little by little. Oh, there the servant has gone and opened the veranda door, and let in a whole flood of sunshine.
MISS TESMAN: Well, then we will shut it.
HEDDA: No no, not that! Tesman, please draw the curtains. That will give a softer light.
TESMAN: All right—all right.—There now, Hedda, now you have both shade and fresh air.
HEDDA: Yes, fresh air we certainly must have, with all these stacks of flowers—. But—won't you sit down, Miss Tesman?
MISS TESMAN: No, thank you. Now that I have seen that everything is all right here—thank heaven!—I must be getting home again. My sister is lying longing for me, poor thing.
TESMAN: Give her my very best love, Auntie; and say I shall look in and see her later in the day.
MISS TESMAN: Yes, yes, I'll be sure to tell her. But by-the-bye, George—I had almost forgotten—I have something for you here.

~~TESMAN: What is it, Auntie? Eh?~~
~~MISS TESMAN: Look here, my dear boy.~~
TESMAN: Well, I declare!—Have you really saved them for me, Aunt Julia! Hedda! isn't this touching—eh?
HEDDA: Well, what is it?
TESMAN: My old morning-shoes! My slippers.
HEDDA: Indeed. I remember you often spoke of them while we were abroad.

In this version, we cut to flatten Ibsen's focus on Hedda from the outset. She's less of a force of nature this time.

MISS TESMAN: Good morning, my dear Hedda! Good morning, and a hearty welcome!
HEDDA: Good morning, dear Miss Tesman! ~~So early a call! That is kind of you.~~
MISS TESMAN: Well—has the bride slept well in her new home?
HEDDA: Oh yes, thanks. Passably.
TESMAN: Passably! Come, that's good, Hedda! You were sleeping like a stone when I got up.
HEDDA: Fortunately. ~~Of course, one has always to accustom one's self to new surroundings, Miss Tesman—little by little. Oh, there the servant has gone and opened the veranda door, and let in a whole flood of sunshine.~~
~~MISS TESMAN: Well, then we will shut it.~~
~~HEDDA: No no, not that! Tesman, please draw the curtains. That will give a softer light.~~
~~TESMAN: All right—all right.—There now, Hedda, now you have both shade and fresh air.~~
HEDDA: ~~Yes, fresh air we certainly must have, with all these stacks of flowers—. But~~—won't you sit down, Miss Tesman?
MISS TESMAN: No, thank you. Now that I have seen that everything is all right here—thank heaven!—I must be getting home again. My sister is lying longing for me, poor thing.
TESMAN: Give her my very best love, Auntie; and say I shall look in and see her later in the day.
MISS TESMAN: Yes, yes, I'll be sure to tell her. But by-the-bye, George—I had almost forgotten—I have something for you here.
TESMAN: What is it, Auntie? Eh?
MISS TESMAN: Look here, my dear boy.
TESMAN: Well, I declare!—Have you really saved them for me, Aunt Julia! Hedda! isn't this touching—eh?
~~HEDDA: Well, what is it?~~
TESMAN: My old morning-shoes! My slippers.
~~HEDDA: Indeed. I remember you often spoke of them while we were abroad.~~

Your cut will affect how the audience thinks of particular characters, and whom they consider the core driving force of the show.

Character removal

With very few exceptions, characters exist in the world of a play for a reason. They further a narrative. They can be antagonists, or heroes. Or both. They can bring a message or remind us of a vital piece of news. They play their own minor roles and work toward the larger goal in the overall story. In modern dramaturgy, a character without function is usually a candidate for removal before the end of the first read-through. If you have a play well-regarded enough to have survived hundreds of years, you can assume each character is there for a reason, even if it appears minor. Character removal cuts away their purpose for the production, but can be effective if handled carefully.

Can you tell us about a cut that you ended up regretting?
Ralph Alan Cohen:
In *2 Henry IV*, Mistress Quickly can't stop saying the word "swaggerer." We haven't met Pistol yet. We meet Pistol in [Act] Two [Scene] Four, and then, two scenes later, we meet Shallow. I made the mistake of cutting too much of Shallow. If you have a good Pistol, you want every bit of that buildup, and you want every word, every one of those "swaggerers." The difference with Shallow is we don't know who this person is, and he's coming in with silence. That is a real shot in the arm for the play, and it's also change in pace and tone. That's refreshing. I wanted a two-hour show out of *Henry IV*, not an easy task anyhow. I think I came in at two hours, ten minutes, or two hours, 20. But in order to get there, I lost too much of that Gloucestershire setting. It looks purposeless, not plot driven. "How's so and so?" "Dead, dead. Dead." "How's so-and-so?" "Oh, dead." All those characters are only referred to. You don't know them at all. The price of cows, all that stuff, none of that is about the story. Now, if you can, a good cut would preserve that. Essentially, it's a change of pace, and a delightful respite. That's coming right halfway through the play. By the end of that scene, we love those guys. We love Shallow, by the end of that scene. So we're going to be very happy to have some more of that respite and some more of those moments of Gloucestershire. Falstaff himself loves it. He doesn't start with that. He doesn't love it at all. He's just come to con the guy. That's all he cares about. And so he's like the audience. He just wants to get on with Plan A, which is the prince. He starts the scene by wanting to leave and just get his thousand pounds. But he stays the night. Then here comes Pistol with the news of the king's death and he's back to Plan A again. But there's this wonderful way in which these boring characters are so delightfully relaxing. If you find yourself in a change of pace thing, don't hurry the change of pace thing.

5.2 Excerpt from interview with Ralph Alan Cohen, 24 November 2020.

Let's look at a few hypotheticals. Remember, at this point, we consider complete excision of characters, if not from the world of the play, then at least from the stage. To illustrate, we propose some hypothetical, evocative, *indefensible* cuts.

Say, for example, you stage *Hamlet*, and you need to trim your cast. Who can you cut? Let's start low and work up. What about Barnardo and Francisco? Palace guards, only a handful of lines. Except those lines are vital reportage on the ghost of king Hamlet: without their report, how does Horatio come to the ramparts to see the Ghost? Without Horatio's access to Hamlet, how does the prince discover what's amiss? No, you need those guards. Trim them back a little, but you need them.

What about messengers? Okay, but what message do they provide? Cornelius and Voltemand appear only twice: as they are sent to Norway and when they come back again. Sure, you could cut those two, but then you lose a major reference to the conflict between Fortinbras and Old Hamlet, which cuts the legs out from under young Fortinbras's march to Poland and his Act V invasion. Indeed, Fortinbras was long a cut victim—Olivier removed him entirely to ensure Hamlet's death was the play's very last moment. Without Fortinbras, Denmark ends the play leaderless and alone. Historically, Rosencrantz and Guildenstern were often some of the first cuts from early productions. They could be replaced by nameless servants who bring Hamlet to Claudius and the only loss was their ultimately futile avenue to Hamlet's past. Then Tom Stoppard came along. The smash Edinburgh Festival Fringe success of *Rosencrantz and Guildenstern are Dead* in 1966 made two hapless fools crucial to the audience's enjoyment. You could cut *one* of them, or even merge them, but their fame draws the audience's attention to the fact that a change has been made.

What about the Polonius family? Without Polonius's death, Ophelia doesn't go mad. Nor does Laertes come back in a rage. Without Ophelia, we lose one of the very few female roles and Hamlet's confrontation at the gravesite is toothless. Without Laertes, there's no one to plot with Claudius or poison Hamlet. No, we can't do without any of them.

Gertrude? She's the emotional fulcrum of the entire play: her too-fast remarriage is as big a sore point for Hamlet as his father's death or his own thwarted ambition. Without Gertrude's calm influence on both her new husband and her son, the play goes off the rails much sooner. Claudius? Cut him and there's no conflict at all. Forget it.

The Players can be cut or merged (the Priam and Hecuba speech is often a goner) but you need them so Hamlet can set the Mousetrap. You can merge gravediggers, but you need at least one to hand Hamlet Yorick's skull, so this lonely laborer has to sadly talk to himself beforehand. Osric could be cut, but the wager on the duel between Hamlet and Laertes represents important context.

Clearly, *Hamlet* is a well-constructed play which makes great use of its characters, even seemingly insignificant ones. As such, complete character removal is problematic because just about every character has a storytelling purpose. Can you trim them back so they still exist in the world of the play but shift to the periphery or off-stage? Could you do *Hamlet* without Hamlet?

This is an actual question asked of us in the past, when a director of esteem proposed an adaptation of *Hamlet* in which the title character did not appear. "What if," he asked, "we cut every line Hamlet speaks, always with the idea that he is in the next room, being spoken of. We'll call it *Hamless*." Groan-worthy joke aside, the concept intrigued Toby enough to give it a spin. *Can* you try a *Hamlet* without Hamlet? Do the moments between Claudius and Polonius work when not balanced out by Hamlet's perspective? Can Horatio hold up his side of the bargain without the prince? And just to be clear, Hamlet still *exists* in this world: he just never *appears*. Can our audience follow based *purely* on prior knowledge of what is supposed to happen?

It turns out Hamlet is quite important to *Hamlet*. Far more than any of the characters we mentioned above, Hamlet pervades every corner of his play. Without his soliloquies, we lose the vitality of his inner thoughts. If Hamlet is gone, the forward momentum of the world screeches to a halt, even if we establish Hamlet as just out of earshot, or redistribute his lines as reportage. The play finds its best point of momentum after Hamlet's banishment to England, but as soon as he returns, he doesn't leave the stage again, making it tricky to engineer his death off stage. This futile exercise demonstrates that for the most part, playwrights know exactly what they are doing when they create narrative structure. Cutting within them will create something new. You could *try Hamless*, but it's a different play, more experimental than interpretive.

Lesser-known plays, particularly classics with enormous casts but little audience recognition, offer better opportunities for this kind of character excision.

Maxim Gorky's *The Lower Depths* (1901) features a remarkable cast of 17 named characters alongside innumerable anonymous figures who populate the central homeless shelter set. Even with characters doubled, any production requires a company with large enough resources to cast 15 or more actors. What's more, several figures appear only sporadically, to emphasize the ensemble style. A cut of *The Lower Depths* might focus the audience on certain stories, such as the fortunes of the pilgrim Luka or the luckless thief Pepel. To remove other stories changes the direction of a given scene, and can reformulate the narrative thrust, so cut carefully.

Say, for example, your COVID-set adaptation of *The Lower Depths* wants to avoid the question of class. When the play was written, class was a vital, central element, and would become even more important as 1917 loomed. As such, The Baron, who represented the fallen aristocracy ruined by the emancipation of the serfs, was a pivotal figure as a man once used to the higher echelons of society now reduced to pimp the unfortunate Nastya. Now let's suggest our hypothetical class-conservative company wishes to cut the Baron to reduce this story. Can it work?

Let's be very clear right off the bat. Cutting the Baron's story changes the play. It removes texture and conflict, but also shifts focus to other stories. Most of the Baron's action is part of the ensemble, so interjections and arguments can be reassigned. Major plot elements can be singled out and lifted entirely. We see here (from Jenny Covan's 1922 public domain translation) a confrontation between the Baron and Pepel, which gives texture and perspective on his fall from grace, but no structural information necessary to the remainder of the work.

LUKA: Who do they say feels dreary?
PEPEL: I do.
   [The Baron enters.]
LUKA: Well, well—out there in the kitchen there's a girl reading and crying! That's so! Her eyes are wet with tears... I say to her: "What's the matter, darling?" And she says: "It's so sad!" "What's so sad?" say I. "The book!" says she.—And that's how people spend their time. Just because they're bored...
THE BARON: She's a fool!
PEPEL: Have you had tea, Baron?
THE BARON: Yes. Go on!
PEPEL: Well—want me to open a bottle?
THE BARON: Of course. Go on!
PEPEL: Drop on all fours, and bark like a dog!
THE BARON: Fool! What's the matter with you? Are you drunk?
PEPEL: Go on—bark a little! It'll amuse me. You're an aristocrat. You didn't even consider us human formerly, did you?
THE BARON: Go on!
PEPEL: Well—and now I am making you bark like a dog—and you will bark, won't you?
THE BARON: All right. I will. You jackass! What pleasure can you derive from it since I myself know that I have sunk almost lower than you. You should have made me drop on all fours in the days when I was still above you.
BUBNOFF: That's right...
LUKA: I say so, too!
BUBNOFF: What's over, is over. Remain only trivialities. We know no class distinctions here. We've shed all pride and self-respect. Blood and bone—man—just plain man—that's what we are!
LUKA: In other words, we're all equal... and you, friend, were you really a Baron?
THE BARON: Who are you? A ghost?
LUKA: *[laughing]* I've seen counts and princes in my day—this is the first time I meet a baron—and one who's decaying—at that!
PEPEL: *[laughing]* Baron, I blush for you!
THE BARON: It's time you knew better, Vassily ...

LUKA: Hey-hey—I look at you, brothers—the life you're leading …
BUBNOFF: Such a life! As soon as the sun rises, our voices rise, too—in quarrels!
THE BARON: We've all seen better days—yes! I used to wake up in the morning and drink my coffee in bed—coffee—with cream! Yes—
LUKA: And yet we're all human beings. Pretend all you want to, put on all the airs you wish, but man you were born, and man you must die. And as I watch I see that the wiser people get, the busier they get—and though from bad to worse, they still strive to improve—stubbornly—
THE BARON: Who are you, old fellow? Where do you come from?
LUKA: I?
THE BARON: Are you a tramp?
LUKA: We're all of us tramps—why—I've heard said that the very earth we walk on is nothing but a tramp in the universe.
THE BARON: *[severely]* Perhaps. But have you a passport?
LUKA: *[after a short pause]* And what are you—a police inspector?
PEPEL: *[delighted]* You scored, old fellow! Well, Barosha, you got it this time!
BUBNOFF: Yes—our little aristocrat got his!
THE BARON: *[embarrassed]* What's the matter? I was only joking, old man. Why, brother, I haven't a passport, either.
BUBNOFF: You lie!
THE BARON: Oh—well—I have some sort of papers—but they have no value—
LUKA: They're papers just the same—and no papers are any good—
PEPEL: Baron—come on to the saloon with me—
THE BARON: I'm ready. Good-bye, old man—you old scamp—
LUKA: Maybe I am one, brother—
PEPEL: *[near doorway]* Come on—come on!
    [Leaves, Baron following him quickly.]
LUKA: Was he really once a Baron?
BUBNOFF: Who knows? A gentleman—? Yes. That much he's even now. Occasionally it sticks out. He never got rid of the habit.
LUKA: Nobility is like small-pox. A man may get over it—but it leaves marks …
BUBNOFF: He's all right all the same—occasionally he kicks—as he did about your passport …
    [Alyoshka comes in, slightly drunk, with a concertina in his hand, whistling.]
ALYOSHKA: Hey there, lodgers!

The episodic nature of the naturalist play means scenes can be trimmed and stray lines can be reassigned. Here, the Baron's entire interaction can be lifted out, as we seamlessly move the audience from one episode to the next.

LUKA: Who do they say feels dreary?
PEPEL: I do.

[Alyoshka comes in, slightly drunk, with a concertina in his hand, whistling.]
ALYOSHKA: Hey there, lodgers!

Of course, the relationships in the play are compromised: the class-centric mockery, the variety of voices in the room, and Nastya's dependence are all impacted. But the play can still run. Remove an entire character, even as an exercise, and you might better understand the character's role in the piece.

Other characters exist in the periphery for a reason. They support the main action, and while they often contribute to the narrative or resolution of the piece, they are a go-to opportunity for line trims. We rarely set out to actively remove a full character, yet it is an option in the toolkit. Can your play manage without a figure? Usually, no. But sometimes…

Character conflation

Character cuts aren't always a matter of body removal. Often, when a minor figure is cut, necessary lines are left behind, which you can reassign to another character. You must do this carefully, but if your play features two attendants in the same scene, you might cut the second attendant, with their necessary lines passed to their compatriot, without major damage. This process, which we'll refer to as *conflation*, can clarify a scene.

Let's reiterate, though: characters appear because the playwright needed them for a reason. However, the playwright's reason might not be the same as *yours*. A minor role may be pivotal, but maybe it's a character role written to fulfill the needs of the original company—or to give a role to the company manager's brother-in-law. The personnel conditions of those original productions are likely different from yours.

Rarely will you cut a character and make your production *more* nuanced. By its nature, this is a process of simplification, often necessary for clarity. We have seen acts of conflation which reduced the run time and line count. A small-cast *Romeo and Juliet* merged Lord and Lady Capulet into one father figure.

> **Kate Mulvany:**
> Even if cutting characters is brutal, sometimes it just makes the story glisten a little more. It's much easier to see the breadcrumbs on the pathway to the gingerbread house than when there's all this detritus of other characters, who would have been more recognizable to Shakespearean audiences, but to us, they've just been lost in time.

5.3 Excerpt from interview with Kate Mulvany, 14 February 2021.

This conflation brought up an interestingly intimate relationship between Capulet and the Nurse, but also meant Capulet's explosive reaction to Juliet's refusal to wed Paris lost multiple layers of context. The loss of Lady Capulet removed an important maternal connection (or lack thereof), and rendered Juliet's final death tableau hollow, without a moment of shared grief.

Aili, working with a company that prefers to keep the cast size below 12, found conflation helpful in her production of *The Duchess of Malfi*, a play overpopulated with easy-to-merge courtiers. Although conflating them minimizes some of the complex constellations of court intrigue, an audience unfamiliar with the play may welcome this simplification. Take this section of Act Five, Scene Four. Four courtiers enter in attendance to the Cardinal, promise they will not come to his aid if they hear him shout, and then discuss the weather:

> *An apartment in the residence of the Cardinal and Ferdinand.*
> *Enter Cardinal, Pescara, Malatesti, Roderigo, and Grisolan.*

CARDINAL:
You shall not watch to-night by the sick prince;
His grace is very well recovered.

MALATESTI:
Good my lord, suffer us.

CARDINAL:
     O, by no means;
The noise, and change of object in his eye,
Doth more distract him: I pray, all to bed;
And though you hear him in his violent fit,
Do not rise, I entreat you.

PESCARA:
     So, sir; we shall not.

CARDINAL:
Nay, I must have you promise
Upon your honours, for I was enjoin'd to 't
By himself; and he seem'd to urge it sensibly.

PESCARA:
Let our honours bind this trifle.

CARDINAL:
Nor any of your followers.

MALATESTI:
     Neither.

CARDINAL:
It may be, to make trial of your promise,
When he 's asleep, myself will rise and feign
Some of his mad tricks, and cry out for help,
And feign myself in danger.

MALATESTI:
>If your throat were cutting,
I'd not come at you, now I have protested against it.
CARDINAL:
Why, I thank you.

Withdraws to the upper end of the apartment.

GRISOLAN:
'Twas a foul storm to-night.
RODERIGO:
The Lord Ferdinand's chamber shook like an osier.
MALATESTI:
'Twas nothing but pure kindness in the devil
To rock his own child.

Exeunt all except the Cardinal.

When we conflate Roderigo with Grisolan and Malatesti with Pescara, we have fewer people to juggle on the stage, and can remove some of the repeated promises:

An apartment in the residence of the Cardinal and Ferdinand.

Enter Cardinal, Pescara, ~~Malatesti,~~ Roderigo, ~~and Grisolan~~.

CARDINAL:
You shall not watch to-night by the sick prince;
His grace is very well recovered.
~~MALATESTI.~~ PESCARA:
Good my lord, suffer us.
CARDINAL:
>O, by no means;
The noise, and change of object in his eye,
Doth more distract him: I pray, all to bed;
And though you hear him in his violent fit,
Do not rise, I entreat you.
PESCARA:
>So, sir; we shall not.
~~CARDINAL:~~
~~Nay, I must have you promise~~
~~Upon your honours, for I was enjoin'd to 't~~
~~By himself; and he seem'd to urge it sensibly.~~
~~PESCARA:~~
~~Let our honours bind this trifle.~~
CARDINAL:
Nor any of your followers.
~~MALATESTI.~~ PESCARA:
>Neither.

CARDINAL:
> It may be, to make trial of your promise,
> When he 's asleep, myself will rise and feign
> Some of his mad tricks, and cry out for help,
> And feign myself in danger.

~~MALATESTI.~~ PESCARA:
>   If your throat were cutting,
> I'd not come at you, now I have protested against it.

CARDINAL:
> Why, I thank you.

Withdraws to the upper end of the apartment.

~~GRISOLAN.~~ RODERIGO:
> 'Twas a foul storm to-night.

~~RODERIGO:~~
> The Lord Ferdinand's chamber shook like an osier.

~~MALATESTI.~~ PESCARA:
> 'Twas nothing but pure kindness in the devil
> To rock his own child.

Exeunt all except the Cardinal.

In the context of this brief scene, the gains in terms of time are minor, yet they add up when carried out through the course of the play. An audience would be hard-pressed to keep track of each specific minor attendant's journey in this text. A careful read reveals personality traits to distinguish them from cardboard courtiers, yet to blend them simplifies the story, lowers the cast size, and relieves some of the crowding a director has to manage on a small stage. The improvements in time are an incidental benefit.

Consequences

Conflations can have consequences. For example, a curiously common *Twelfth Night* character conflation merges the clown character of Feste with the gentleman Fabian. Feste is a licensed fool who sings in the houses of nobility, quips for change, and revels with the clowns. Feste is an enduring character, with the wisdom to comment on the action but enough sense to stay far away.

 As Sir Toby and Maria scheme about a false letter to trick Malvolio, Feste steps to one side, curiously silent about the plot and scheme, and by the time the letter is dropped, Feste is gone. He is replaced by Fabian, a new character who appears for the first time in this crucial scene. Fabian participates in a trick on Malvolio and remains complicit throughout the rest of play.

 Fabian and Feste share the stage on multiple occasions, but never converse in any meaningful way. So, as a conservative effort, one solution is to cut

Fabian entirely from the production and to assign his lines to Feste. The alliterative connection between the character names seems neat, so to merge these characters and place Feste squarely inside the scheme is a clear possibility.

Is it really so simple? Can we simply reassign lines in such a cavalier manner? Changes like this have repercussions, which begin immediately when we consider character. Fabian and Feste are nothing alike. Feste is the witty licensed fool; Fabian is, by his manner of speech, significantly higher born, arguably closer in rank to Sir Toby than to Feste. He is variously described as a "magistrate," a "justice of the peace," an "esquire," and "gentleman" (Breuer 441), although he is often portrayed onstage as a servant on the same level as Maria. Shakespeare introduces him abruptly toward the end of Act II:

SIR TOBY: Come thy ways, Signor Fabian.
FABIAN: Nay, I'll come! If I lose a scruple of this sport, let me be boiled to death with melancholy.
SIR TOBY: Wouldst thou not be glad to have the niggardly rascally sheep-biter come by some notable shame?
FABIAN: I would exult, man! You know he brought me out o'favor with my lady, about a bear-baiting here.

This is clearly a different person from the clever Feste, a higher-born figure, out of favor with Olivia over a bear-baiting. Thoughtlessly merging these characters with little in common beyond a shared "F" name and association with Sir Toby is risky. The inherent outsider, Feste, is no longer simply an observer who comments on the action; he is guilty as he aids and abets the dropping of the letter in front of Malvolio. Even though he later participates under the guise of Sir Topas the curate, disguise offers him customary distance. Feste's complicity means he has chosen a side rather than being counsel to all. Add the difference in speech styles and you find yourself with an uncomfortable melange where Feste speaks in his own voice along with the borrowed text from Fabian.

Beware the undermined or under-developed

As you cut, even without conflation or character elimination, you must attend character development. Sometimes, we cut lines because they don't move the *story* forward, and only realize much later those lines were for the purpose of *character*, rather than narrative. Without them, you lose track of what kind of person a character is, which drives their choices and powers the narrative.

Unfortunately, such problems are often imperceptible until the work is on its feet. Christine Schmidle told us about her time working as a text associate in rehearsals for a conflated *Henry VI*. The daunting task was to fit a three-play conflation into a reasonable run time, so they chose to cut two large scenes from Eleanor and Gloucester. In rehearsal, the team realized these characters' relationship didn't make much sense without the absent text.

"We had the skeleton, but we didn't have the human being anymore... I think that's easier to see if you haven't done the cuts yourself." They restored some of the lines to develop the characters more deeply.

Some characters exist entirely to allow the core characters to show their depth. In Alice Dunbar-Nelson's one-act play *Mine Eyes Have Seen* (1918), the focal character is a young Black man, Chris, who has just learned that he has been drafted into the army. The action of the play consists of visitors stopping by, hearing the news, offering a sentence or two of their own perspective, and receiving Chris and his family's reaction. Although they each have only a line or two, without any of them, we would miss seeing Chris' conflicting feelings, from anger at how Black people have fought to defend a country that refused to give them equal rights, to guilt over leaving his dependent siblings, to patriotic love of his country, despite its flaws. Cutting or conflating some of them would be easy, but would sacrifice the opportunity to explore Chris' conundrum.

Care for characters

You should consider character in all cuts: trim important details, and you might complicate the actor's preparation and confuse the audience. Merge or snip characters with an eye to company efficiency, but neglect to think of the wider-reaching effects, and you risk greater problems down the line.

Works cited

Breuer, Horst. "Shakespeare's Signior Fabian". *English Studies* 74:5 (1993), pp. 441–444. https://doi.org/10.1080/00138389308598876

6 Don't Cut That! The Mechanics of Cuts

In some cuts, we need to amputate large chunks of text, maybe even entire scenes. If we assume the story will withstand these large excisions, these cuts can be relatively easy to make. A more precise and pickier sort of cut, but one less likely to be detected even by an audience familiar with the script, involves snips to remove tiny bits out of the midst of lines. One challenge with this type of cut is preserving the playwright's unique voice. Playwrights use rhetoric, meter, and rhyme to shape the world and its characters. In this chapter, we look at these structures, embedded in every line, and make a plan to preserve the essential character in a shortened text.

The first step is to understand how the playwright has structured the language and the tools these structures offer to the actor. The most important of these are *meter, rhetoric,* and *diction.*

Meter

Verse cuts can feel daunting; so much of what compels in verse dramas is the heartbeat of the verse. If you pick it apart, how can you stitch it back together and get it to tick again? Before we can take it apart, let's start with a simple question: "What is verse?"

Verse simply means a set rhythmic pattern which repeats. The playwright sometimes shifts or disrupts this pattern. The best verse writers run jazz riffs on top of that steady beat. The exact structure of the verse varies from playwright to playwright and throughout history. Most readers are familiar with the iambic pentameter popular in Elizabethan theatrical verse, but other periods had their own verse forms.

Let's begin with a quick review of basic verse terminology. In English, as well as German, Russian, and other stress-timed languages, specific syllables of words are *stressed*, while others are *unstressed*. We can most easily hear the difference between stressed and unstressed syllables with words identical except for this stress (called *scansion*).

Say this aloud: "Let's record a record!"

vicious **plague**   **dele**terious **plague**
      1   2

6.1 Unstressed syllables move slowly when they come as single spies, but rush along in battalions.

You can hear that the verb has the stress on the second syllable: re**cord**. The noun has it on the first syllable: **re**cord. All multisyllabic English words have stressed and unstressed syllables.

The stressed syllables are essentially the metronome for the verse. When we say a language is *stress-timed*, this means the stressed syllables get equal emphasis, and have a consistent space of time between them. The unstressed syllables compress to preserve this timing.

Here's another set of phrases to say aloud (or better, ask someone to read it to you so you can hear the timing): "Vicious plague." "Deleterious plague."

Did you notice how much more quickly the unstressed syllables in the end of *deleterious* zip by, compared to the last, unstressed syllable of *vicious*? This is because you instinctively understand how English is supposed to sound, so you preserve the space between stressed syllables, no matter how many unstressed syllables come between them.

When you cut a verse play, maintain the number of stressed syllables in a line. You can get away with an occasional short line where the playwright didn't have one, but too many and the verse starts to sound like it has a square wheel. Be aware that the *sentence* or *thought* might extend past the end of the line. This is called an enjambed line, and it can make a cut more of a challenge.

Let's compare lines from John Webster's *The Duchess of Malfi* (1613). The outset of Webster's career overlapped with the end of Shakespeare's, and he clearly learned from Shakespeare's late-career expansive verse. Webster uses a lot of enjambed lines.

In this section, the Duchess tries to convince her steward she loves him. He insists he's unworthy of her.

> The misery of us that are born great!
> We are forc'd to woo, because none dare woo us;
> And as a tyrant doubles with his words,
> And fearfully equivocates, so we
> Are forc'd to express our violent passions
> In riddles and in dreams, and leave the path
> Of simple virtue, which was never made
> To seem the thing it is not. Go, go brag
> You have left me heartless; mine is in your bosom:

Notice the different thoughts in this passage, marked below with different fonts.

> The misery of us that are born great!
> `We are forc'd to woo, because none dare woo us;`

> And as a tyrant doubles with his words,
> And fearfully equivocates, so we
> Are forc'd to express our violent passions
> In riddles and in dreams, and leave the path
> Of simple virtue, which was never made
> To seem the thing it is not. Go, go brag
> You have left me heartless; mine is in your bosom:

Either of those first lines could easily be removed and not alter the course of the meter. Both thoughts end with the verse line. They give the actor a lot of meaty, direct language to work with, though. If we take them out, the audience has to guess that what the Duchess wants to communicate is what she says so clearly in the second line. That line holds the conflict of the whole speech—the whole scene. The heavily-enjambed section with the tyrant is clearly a digression, but if we slice it out whole cloth, we're left with a short and awkward line on "Go, go brag…"

Aili's production cut of this speech looks like this, which takes advantage of the irregularity of the verse lines in this speech overall:

> The misery of us that are born great!
> We are forc'd to woo, because none dare woo us;
> ~~And as a tyrant doubles with his words,~~
> ~~And fearfully equivocates, so we~~
> Are forc'd to express our violent passions
> In riddles and in dreams, ~~and leave the path~~
> ~~Of simple virtue, which was never made~~
> ~~To seem the thing it is not.~~ Go, go brag
> You have left me heartless; mine is in your bosom:

Here's another cut which goes further. It misses the sense of "Go, go brag you have left me heartless," and turns the sentiment from a command into a lament:

> The misery of us that are born great!
> We are forc'd to woo, because none dare woo us;
> ~~And as a tyrant doubles with his words,~~
> ~~And fearfully equivocates, so we~~
> ~~Are forc'd to express our violent passions~~
> ~~In riddles and in dreams, and leave the path~~
> ~~Of simple virtue, which was never made~~
> ~~To seem the thing it is not. Go, go brag~~
> You have left me heartless; mine is in your bosom:

Anglophone playwrights use the inherent rhythms of the language to create character. Some characters have a lot of unstressed syllables to cram between their stresses, which makes them seem hurried, rushed, intense. Other characters have a lot of space in their lines, and land on big open vowels with taps of unstressed syllables in between, like skipping a stone across a pond. Some characters' verse ticks along like a watch, with a steady and unchanging *stressed unstressed stressed unstressed* beat. Other characters' verse wiggles and dodges: they check in with the core meter from time to time, but sound unstable and uncertain as they meander. These qualities are one way the playwright tells us about a character. If we happen to have a character whose lines are occasionally regular, but more often are not, we want to be careful in our cuts to favor the lines which wander, because those are the ones that align the actor's voice with the character's mind.

While early Elizabethan dramas can be dogmatic in their commitment to regularity, by the Jacobean period, the verse became more flexible and able to specify character. Webster's characters rarely speak in successions of perfect five-beat lines, but the proportion of their regular lines clearly reflects their character or their present frame of mind.

In *The Duchess of Malfi*, a widowed Duchess marries her household steward, Antonio, in secret. When her brothers find out, they are furious, because they had planned to force her into a politically advantageous marriage. In this first speech, Ferdinand has barged into his sister's chambers, in the hope he will catch her with her beloved. He still doesn't know the man's identity. Antonio flees just in time. Listen to how clear Ferdinand's intention is in these lines, which are nearly all regular, or spill over into an unstressed ending, a Webster hallmark.

FERDINAND:

> What**e'er** thou **art** that **hast** en**joy**ed my **sis**ter,
> For **I** am **sure** thou **hear'st** me, for **thine** own **sake**
> **Let** me not **know** thee. **I** came **hi**ther pre**pared**
> To **work** thy dis**cov**'ry; **yet** am **now** per**suad**ed
> It **would** be**get** such **vio**lent **ef**fects
> As would **damn** us **both**. I **would** not **for** ten **mil**lions
> I **had** be**held** thee: **there**fore **use** all **means**
> I **nev**er **may** have **know**ledge **of** thy **name**

By contrast, note his confusion, both in thought and verse, when several scenes later he learns his sister has married so far below her station.

FERDINAND:

> An**ton**io!
> A **slave** that **on**ly **smelled** of **ink** and **count**ers,
> And never in 's **life** look'd **like** a **gent**leman,
> **But** in the **aud**it-**time**. **Go**, go **pres**ently,
> **Draw** me **out** an **hun**dred and **fif**ty of our **horse**,
> And **meet** me **at** the **foot**-bridge.

As we cut, we try, when possible, to preserve the pounding regular lines in the earlier scene, but eschew them in favor of the muddled lines in the latter.

If we identify how verse patterns help tell the story of the scene, we can ensure our cuts preserve that story tool.

Each play has its own internal logic. As playwrights hone their craft through the course of their careers, their use of verse evolves. To determine whether an irregular verse line communicates information on the character, look for irregularity in the context of the whole play. You may have noticed that even in the more regular set of lines, we have several unstressed endings. The conventional wisdom about unstressed endings is that they make a character seem to waver or feel unstable (think of the most uncertain of characters, Hamlet, whose most famous line ends in an unstressed syllable: "To **be** or **not** to **be**, that **is** the **ques**tion."). Whether it has this effect in a specific play depends on the context of the other lines. Webster loves to write lines which burst at the seams. Nearly every character has a significant number of lines that overflow the measure. In the first example, about a third of Ferdinand's lines have an extra syllable. While that would be a lot for an early Shakespeare play, it's about par for Webster. But notice how much *more* unstable the verse is in our second example. Not only does it have unstressed syllables ending nearly every line, but some lines end with *two* unstressed syllables (***gentleman***, ***presently***). Because Webster's lines frequently have an extra syllable, they need even more turbulence to convey the shock Ferdinand feels in this latter scene.

Verse can also tell us about the relationship between characters. Some characters share lines, where one has the first two beats of the line, but the other has the completing three. These shared lines primarily appear in scenes between lovers or enemies: shared lines ramp up the energy of their passionate connection. In *Duchess*, both types of shared lines appear in a single minute of stage time. Bosola, who works for the Duchess' wicked brother, pursues her and her husband as they flee their palace. He catches up with them just as the two lovers have shared their inmost fears about their situation. Note how Webster even here has his verse extend past the line a bit.

DUCHESS:
   I had a very strange dream to-night.
ANTONIO:
   What was 't?
DUCHESS:
               Methought I wore my coronet of state,
   And on a sudden all the diamonds
   Were changed to pearls.
ANTONIO:
                      My interpretation
   Is, you'll weep shortly; for to me the pearls
   Do signify your tears.
DUCHESS:
                   The birds that live i' the field
   On the wild benefit of nature live
   Happier than we; for they may choose their mates,

And carol their sweet pleasures to the spring.
Enter Bosola with a letter.
BOSOLA: You are happily o'erta'en.
DUCHESS:
                              From my brother?
BOSOLA:
   Yes, from the Lord Ferdinand, your brother,
   All love and safety.
DUCHESS:
                    Thou dost blanch mischief,
   Would'st make it white. See, see, like to calm weather
   At sea before a tempest, false hearts speak fair
   To those they intend most mischief.

If we cut this section for time, we'd preserve at least some of those shared lines. They tell the actors to keep the rhythm tight, they intensify the connection between the characters, and they communicate to the audience this sense of how they finish each other's sentences.

We might do something like this:

DUCHESS:
   I had a very strange dream to-night.
ANTONIO:
   What was 't?
DUCHESS:
                  Methought I wore my coronet of state,
   And on a sudden all the diamonds
   Were changed to pearls.
ANTONIO:
                        My interpretation
   Is, you'll weep shortly; ~~for to me the pearls~~
   ~~Do signify your tears.~~
DUCHESS:
                          The birds that live i' the field
   On the wild benefit of nature live
   Happier than we; for they may choose their mates,
   And carol their sweet pleasures to the spring.
Enter Bosola with a letter.
BOSOLA:
   You are happily o'erta'en.
DUCHESS:
                        From my brother?
BOSOLA:
   Yes, from the Lord Ferdinand, your brother,
   All love and safety.
DUCHESS:
                     Thou dost blanch mischief

> ~~Would'st make it white. See, see, like to calm weather~~
> ~~At sea before a tempest, false hearts speak fair~~
> ~~To those they intend most mischief.~~

You'll notice, in the cut in Antonio's line, the half-line which pairs with the Duchess' is cut—but what remains of his line is a half-line, so neither line is left hanging. In some ways, this cut makes the relationship between Antonio and the Duchess even more intimate. He doesn't have to say much at all for her to understand and complete his thoughts. Her accusation to Bosola may feel even more powerful in its brevity.

Rhyme

One other key feature of verse is that some of it rhymes. One mark of a carelessly cut script is one sprinkled with incomplete rhymes. Not all verse rhymes, and sometimes a playwright leaves a rhyme hanging on purpose. Care with rhymes can make a cut seamless. We'll mostly focus on end-rhymes; although internal rhymes add to the texture of the words, they generally aren't as obvious when they're cut.

As you cut a rhymed passage, the first step is to identify the rhyme scheme, or pattern. Here's a straight-forward example: Death, from the Anonymous *Everyman* (c.1510, but cited here from the 1535 published text).

> Lorde I wyll in the worlde go renouer all
> And truely out serche bothe great and small
> Eueryman I wyll be set that lyueth beestly
> Out of goddes lawes / and dredeth not foly
> He that loueth ryches I wyll stryke with my darte
> His syght to blynde / and from heuen depart.

To make it easier to work with, let's modernize the spelling and phrasing a little.

> Lord, I will in the world go run over all
> And truly out search both great and small.
> Everyman will I beset that liveth beastly
> Out of God's laws and dreadeth not folly.
> He that loveth riches, I will strike w' my dart,
> His sight to blind and for heaven depart.

Death's rhyme scheme is a series of couplets: AABBCC, and on and on. All of his lines have this pattern. To cut down his speech, an inelegant choice would be to excise one half of a rhymed pair, but leave the other one. This cut, for example, highlights what is lost in this poor choice:

> Lord, I will in the world go run over all
> Every man will I beset that liveth beastly

84   *Don't Cut That! The Mechanics of Cuts*

> He that loveth riches, I will strike w' my dart,
> His sight to blind and for heaven depart.

You *could* cut all of Death's lines to hide the rhymes, but the medieval poets loved their end-rhymes. A less-rhymed *Everyman* feels divorced from its historical context.

A better cut might look like this:

> Lord, I will in the world go run over all
> And truly out search both great and small.
> He that loveth riches, I will strike w' my dart,
> His sight to blind and for heaven depart.

Here's a more complex rhyme scheme from the Wakefield Master's *The Second Shepherd's Play* (c.1500):

MAK:

> Now crys holy name: be vs emang
> What is thus for sant Iame: I may not well gang
> I trow I be the same: A my nek has lygen wrang
> ----------Enoghe
> Mekill thank syn yister euen// Now by sant strevyn
> I was flayd with a swevyn my hart out of sloghe

Once more, let's modernize the spelling and formatting a little for clarity.

MAK:

> Now Christ's holy name be us amang,
> What is thus? for Saint James!–I may not well gang.
> I trow I be the same. Ah! my neck has lain wrang
> Enough
> Mickle thank, since yester-even
> Now, by Saint Stephen!
> I was flayed with a sweven, –
> My heart out of slough.

The rhyme pattern here is AAABCCCB, which means the first three lines (A) rhyme, then there's a one-off that seems not to rhyme anywhere (B), then three more lines which rhyme with each other (C), and at last, the completion of the B rhyme. The B rhyme is also a good example of a pair of words that rhyme on the page, but not to the ear. Pronunciation shifts over time, and how to handle obsolete rhymes is a question beyond the scope of this work. Suffice to note that "enough" and "slough" rhymed for the author 500 years ago, and treat them, for the purposes of your cut, as if they still do. If you want cuts to preserve the consistency of the rhyme for your audience, try to cut those outdated rhymes as much as you can, while maintaining the sense of the text, to circumvent a rehearsal room debate over how to pronounce them.

With a rhyme pattern so intricately entwined, cuts can be a challenge. Luckily, the doggerel verse of the Wakefield Master doesn't have a specific number of rhymes for each ending. They roll on until they run out. Mak's line continues:

> I thoght gyll began to crok: and trauell full sad
> Welner at the fyrst cuf: of a yong lad
> For to mend oure flok: then be I neuer glad
> I haue tow on my rok: more then euer I had
> ----------A my heede
> A house full of yong tharmes// The dewill knok outt thare harnes
> Wo is hym has many barnes// And therto lytyll brede

Or, in modern tones:

> I thought Gill began to croak, and travail full sad,
> Well nigh at the first cock, –of a young lad,
> For to mend our flock: then be I never glad.
> To have two on my rock, –more than ever I had.
> Ah, my head!
> A house full of young tharmes,
> The devil knock out their harnes!
> Woe is he has many bairns,
> And thereto little bread.

So the rhymes can be in pairs, triplets, or quads, and as long as each end rhyme has at least one match, the structure of the rhyme maintains. With this in mind, a reasonable cut might remove Mak's interjections and look like this:

> What is this? for Saint James!–I may not well gang.
> I trust I be the same. Ah! my neck has lain wrang
> Enough
> Mickle thank, since yester-even
> I was flayed with a sweven, –
> My heart out of slough.

Rhetoric

One other important way playwrights create their characters is through rhetoric. Technically, rhythm and rhyme patterns are subsets of rhetoric, but it is useful to consider rhetoric more broadly. Rhetoric is *patterned language*. It can be as specific as the choice of an individual word, or as broad as a character who repeatedly uses logical reasoning in the face of another's appeal to the emotions.

While scholars have named and codified an endless list of rhetorical devices, from *auxesis* to *zeugma*, for practical use, we like to employ a simpler system: "ROADS to Rhetoric." Developed by Cass Morris in her work with the education department at the American Shakespeare Center, ROADS is a mnemonic which outlines the five major types of rhetorical devices: Repetition, Omission, Addition, Direction, and Substitution.

Repetition is simply when sounds, words, or phrases repeat, as in, "Measure for Measure." Rhyme is a form of repetition, as is assonance, as they repeat sounds. Notice the repetition of "Now were time" in Mak's lines from *The Second Shepherd's Play*:

> Now were tyme for a man that lakkys what he wold
> To stalk prevely than unto a fold
> And neemly to wyrk than and be not to bold
> For he myght aby the bargan if it were told
> ----------At the endyng
> Now ere time for to reyll Bot he nedys good counsell
> That fain wold fare weyll And has bot lytyll spendyng

Or, modernized, with the customary adjustment of the second 'Now ere' to 'Now were':

> **Now were time for** a man, that lacks what he wold,
> To stalk privately then into a fold,
> And namely to work then, and be not too bold,
> He might abide the bargain, if it were told
> At the ending.
>
> **Now were time for** to revel;
> But he needs good counsel
> That fain would fare well,
> And has but little spending.

It connects the ideas of the first and second stanzas, allowing them to juxtapose images of working and reveling. Repetition can highlight what is *not* repeated. Repeated phrases create a foil for differences.

Omission is when a character leaves out a sound, word or phrase you would expect to hear, as in Claudius' line: "And he to England shall along with you." Your mind knows that "go" belongs after "shall," but it's not said.

Addition is the opposite, where the playwright adds words or detail beyond what the meaning requires. Take, for example, this insult from *All's Well That Ends Well* which just builds upon itself: "A most notable coward, an infinite

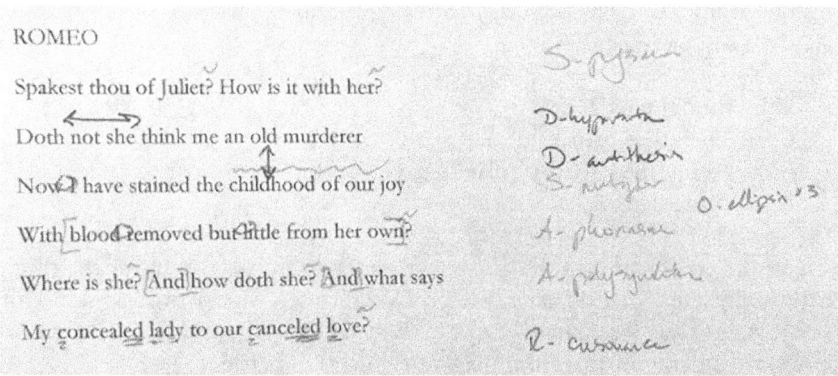

6.2 Everyone develops their own system to mark up rhetoric. Cass Morris shares an example of how she does it.

and endless liar, an hourly promise breaker, the owner of no one good quality." In *The Duchess of Malfi*, Webster uses extra repetitions of "and" to help Bosola emphasize the connection between ranks of men at court: "Fare ye well, sir: and yet do not you scorn us; for places in the court are but like beds in the hospital, where this man's head lies at that man's foot, and so lower and lower."

Direction covers devices that arrange words in order, or, conversely, scramble syntax, as in this speech from *Everyman*:

GOD:
    I perceyue here in my maiestye
    How that all creatures / be to me vnkynde
    Lyuynge without drede / in worldely prosperytye
    Of ghostly syght / the people be so blynde
    Drowned in synne / they know me not for ther god
    In worldely ryches is all theyr mynde.

The syntax here is strange, even for the period; a more normal word order might be: "I perceive here in majesty, how all creatures are unkind to me, living in worldly prosperity without dread. The people are so blind of ghostly sight, drowned in sin. They do not know me for their God. Their mind is all on worldly riches." By reordering the common phrasing, the playwright shifts the most important words or ideas to the ends of the lines, where they can receive the enhanced prominence of end-rhyme. These structures also create tiny moments of suspense: "They know me not—" how? Ah, as their God. What is "in worldly riches"? There it is: the minds of the people. Direction also includes devices which present a contrast. A good example is the opposition of "sight" and "blind," which draws our attention to the importance of these words in that line.

Substitution is any device that swaps out one idea for another. Similes, like this one from *The Duchess of Malfi*, are a common example:

DUCHESS:
    Why should only I,
    Of all the other princes of the world,
    Be cas'd up, **like a holy relic**? I have youth
    And a little beauty.

Sometimes, substitution fully allows an image to fully stand in for the thing that it represents. In *Everyman,* the playwright uses "the sword" to stand for God's vengeance for David's rape of Bathsheba, although this retribution shows up in many forms, from plagues to losses in battle.

PATER CŒLESTIS:
    Thou shalt not die, David, for this iniquity,
    For thy repentance; but thy son by Bathsheba
    Shall die, forasmuch as my name is blasphemed
    Among my enemies, and thou the worse esteemed.
    From thy house **for this the sword shall not depart**.

Personal rhetoric

The way a character uses rhetoric tells us a lot about them as a person. Do they speak directly, or in a round-about manner? Do they use a lot of metaphors in their speech? Do they create lists within lists? When you work on a text cut, take some time to familiarize yourself with the rhetorical patterns specific to each of the characters. Faced with a character who tends to repeat himself, an easy first step is to cut out the repetition—but does that change him as a character? As you cut, make sure you preserve the voice the playwright has given each character. Take a look at Polonius' ramble as he reports an important discovery to the king:

    Have I, my lord? Assure you, my good liege,
    I hold my duty as I hold my soul,
    Both to my God and to my gracious king;
    And I do think—or else this brain of mine
    Hunts not the trail of policy so sure
    As it hath us'd to do—that I have found
    The very cause of Hamlet's lunacy.

It might feel unspeakably tempting to slice thus:

    Have I, my lord? ~~Assure you, my good liege,~~
    ~~I hold my duty as I hold my soul,~~

> ~~Both to my God and to my gracious king;~~
> ~~And I do think—or else this brain of mine~~
> ~~Hunts not the trail of policy so sure~~
> ~~As it hath us'd to do—~~ that I have found
> The very cause of Hamlet's lunacy.

However, to remove all the diversions takes away core components of Polonius' character. Shakespeare wanted him to be exceedingly, maddeningly, slow to reach the point. Cut *some* meandering, sure, but leave enough for Polonius to still sound like Polonius.

Sometimes rhetoric shows us how a character's mind works in real time. Look, for example, at *The Duchess of Malfi*, where Antonio suddenly understands the Duchess wants to marry him:

> Ambition, madam, is a great man's madness,
> That is not kept in chains and close-pent rooms,
> But in fair lightsome lodgings, and is girt
> With the wild noise of prattling visitants,
> Which makes it lunatic beyond all cure.
> Conceive not I am so stupid but I aim
> Whereto your favours tend: but he's a fool
> That, being a-cold, would thrust his hands i' the fire
> To warm them.

Notice the kinds of words he uses and how they change through the course of the speech, as realization dawns on him. He begins with long, formal words: "ambition," "prattling visitants," "close-pent rooms." His last thought, though, is nearly all monosyllabic, as he gets to the core fear of his situation. To love a woman so far above his station is as risky and foolish as to thrust his hands into the fire to warm them up. This progression lets us see his mind work, as he at first tries to politely decline her attentions, then tangles in the middle with a quick and obfuscated admission of mutual affection, only to end with direct language, too overwhelmed to be artful. As we cut this text, we want to do our best to preserve the journey for the actor

Tim Carroll:
I did a production of *Romeo and Juliet* in which I cut quite a lot. I filleted, rather than cutting whole scenes or whole sections, I tried to winnow it away, 5% from every speech or something, and I regretted that. I felt that the scenes felt longer, especially the balcony scene. It felt longer for being five minutes shorter because it didn't just catch you, as

(Continued)

Shakespeare does at his best. [...] It didn't catch you in that completely natural flow where every word in every speech is triggered by a word that has just been spoken. It's not just about preserving the sense of the argument. You often only notice quite late in rehearsal, "Oh, she is picking up on that particular word in that line which *oops*, we've cut, because we didn't need it for the gist." That's the crucial thing—to bear in mind that, until you've *really looked* at a scene, you can't be sure how the words are interacting. You're likely to leave things which make sense, but which are not anchored in something that has just been said. They make sense as generic response, but they don't have the wit of "I'm picking up on that word and throwing back a sentence that has a related word," or the opposite word or whatever. We can all spot it when it's the same word being chucked back, but it's in that later level of rehearsal where you realize, "He's actually taken all three of the things she said, and answered all three of them."

6.3 Excerpt from interview with Tim Carroll, 28 January 2021.

Susannah Centlivre's *A Bold Stroke for a Wife* (1718) contains fantastic examples of how rhetoric can create character. The play's central character is Colonel Fainwell, who falls in love with Ann Lovely. Fainwell has to convince all four of Ann's guardians—a mismatched group of gentlemen—he'd be a suitable husband for her. As Fainwell interacts with each guardian, he changes his rhetoric to match his scene partner's.

Obediah Prim, one of the guardians, is a conservative Quaker. He often says things like, "Friend, thy Garb savoureth too much of the Vanity of the Age for my Approbation; nothing that resembleth Philip Modelove shall I love, mark that —therefore, Friend Philip, bring no more of thy own Apes under my Roof." Fainwell's response to this is, "I am so entirely a Stranger to the Monsters of thy Breed, that I shall bring none of them, I am sure." Fainwell picks up Prim's use of *thy*, which even in Centlivre's time was archaic. He also plays on Prim's use of impenetrable metaphors, using "Monsters of thy Breed" to retort Prim's "thy own Apes." Even audiences unfamiliar with the religious sects of 18th-century England will catch this in their ear; Prim's manner of speech is extremely different from everyone else's in the world of the play.

Later, Fainwell meets Periwinkle, whom Centlivre describes as "a sort of silly virtuoso," and engages in this exchange:

PERIWINKLE:
    What Woman is there, drest in all the Pride and Foppery of the Times, can boast of such a Foretop as the Cockatoor.
COLONEL FAINWELL:
    [*Aside.*] I must humour him.
    Such a Skin as the Lizard?

PERIWINKLE:
   Such a shining Breast as the Humming-Bird?
COLONEL FAINWELL:
   Such a Shape as the Antilope?

To cut this nonsensical exchange feels like an easy win, yet it earns its place in the play. It shows Fainwell's skill as he mimics another's patterns of language. The aside makes clear his intentions. Periwinkle's silliness, key later in the play, is on excellent display, as is his penchant for bizarre simile. Further, the contrast between how Fainwell speaks with Periwinkle as opposed to how he speaks with Prim makes his plan clear to the audience. He's told them earlier, but this is an opportunity to show it in action. In the later scene where he meets Sir Phillip, who excessively uses the word "sir," he hilariously responds in kind. As we cut this section, we must take care to preserve both Sir Phillip's pomposity and Fainwell's imitation of it. We should leave enough in so the "sirs" still feel excessive.

SIR PHILLIP:
   May I presume, Sir?
COLONEL FAINWELL:
   Sir, you honour me. [*Presenting the Snuff Box.*]
SIR PHILLIP:
   He speaks good English—tho' he must be a Foreigner;—this Snuff is
   extremely good—and the Box prodigious fine; the Work is French
   I presume, Sir.
COLONEL FAINWELL:
   I bought it in Paris, Sir, —I do think the Workmanship pretty neat.
SIR PHILLIP:
   Neat! 'tis exquisitely fine, Sir; pray, Sir, if I may take the Liberty of
   inquiring—what Country is so happy to claim the Birth of the finest
   Gentleman in the Universe? France, I presume.

If we have to cut *somewhere*, we will remove some patterned language where a character uses rhetorical structures to build their identity. However, if you are aware of these patterns, you can make more informed and seamless cuts. You don't want unbalanced antitheses or lists which hang in the air like an unresolved chord.

Rhetoric also shows character when lines travel in rhetorical pairs, which complete each other in a manner similar to a rhyme. Notice the paired language in this exchange between Anne Lovely, her maid Betty, her guardian Sir Phillip, Fainwell, and a woman they happen upon in the street.

BETTY:
   Then you don't like the Colonel so well as I thought you did, Madam,
   or you would not **take such a Resolution.**
LOVELY:
   It is because I do like him, Betty, that I **take such a Resolution.**

92   *Don't Cut That! The Mechanics of Cuts*

Sharing what he learned about cutting from his friend and mentor, Stephen Booth, who had passed away a few days before our conversation.
Ralph Alan Cohen:
Booth basically says, 'Quick is good, slow is bad.' He said that in reference to *Macbeth*. He thinks that part of Shakespeare's project in *Macbeth* was to make us like a murderer. One of the ways he does that is to make Macbeth really succinct and really interesting to listen to, with short sentences, and to make Malcolm, who is the alternative to Macbeth really boring and weird. You don't want, for example, the Archbishop of Canterbury to be brief and succinct. Don't clarify Polonius, don't clarify the Duke in *Measure for Measure* in the opening. You know, he's awfully wordy when he talks to the Friar in Act One, Scene Three. It was very wordy, and the friar didn't get to say much, that's the important thing.

6.4 Excerpt from interview with Ralph Alan Cohen, 24 November 2020.

WOMAN:
  I never mind the **Outside** of a Man.
COLONEL FAINWELL:
  And I'm afraid thou art no Judge of the **Inside**.
SIR PHILLIP:
  I am positively of your Mind, Sir. For **Creatures of her Function** seldom penetrate beyond the **Pocket**.
WOMAN:
  Creatures of your Composition have, indeed, generally more in their **Pockets** than in their Heads.

If you cut Betty's first line after "Madam," you kneecap Anne's line which follows it. You *could* cut Fainwell's "And I'm afraid thou art no Judge of the inside," but the Woman's "I never mind the Outside of a Man" would hang unmatched, and scramble the sense of Sir Phillip's next line. The last two lines travel in a matched set: to cut the first would render the second insensible; to cut the second allows the first to stand unchallenged, and make the play less feminist and smart than it is. You might cut the last *four* lines, but only if they all went. To leave any one without the others unbalances the scene's rhetorical back-and-forth.

Pronouns and embedded stage directions

Often, particularly in plays written before easy printing, the playwright did not explicitly write stage directions, but expected the actor to understand what they should do from the dialog. In *Volpone*, when Voltore weeps with contrition, he says, "For which, now struck in conscience, here, I prostate / Myself at your offended feet, for pardon." The magistrates respond: "Arise." We don't need a stage direction to know Voltore kneels, or that he gets up again. If you cut either line, but not both, you may leave your director and actors in a state of confusion. Be aware of what crucial action is included in the text you cut, and if you need to add your own stage direction for the sake of clarity, do so.

Another form of "stage direction" is the particular terms characters use to address each other. In more modern plays, terms of endearment can suggest physical closeness between people onstage. The Elizabethans had another tool to indicate rank and closeness, both physical and emotional. While an 18th-century playwright like Centlivre uses "thee" to mark the speaker as part of a particularly conservative religious sect, in earlier English plays, a character's use of "thee" would indicate they spoke to someone with whom they shared an intimate relationship, or to a child or lower-ranked person. This difference is analogous to formal and informal second person pronouns that exist in many languages, such as French, Spanish, and German. If you are at work on a play in translation from one of these languages, find out which "you" is used, and note it in the script, as a helpful tool to your actors.

Characters in early modern plays use pronouns to invite closeness and to put distance—emotional and physical—between them. In *The Duchess of Malfi*, a subplot involves the Duchess's brother, a Cardinal, and his mistress, the married Julia. In their dialogue, Julia always refers to the Cardinal as "you," which reflects her constant awareness of his rank; no matter how intense their affair, he will always be a Cardinal. He, on the other hand, sometimes refers to her as "thou" and sometimes as "you," as he toys with her. He offers intimacy, and then revokes it.

CARDINAL:
    Sit: **thou** art my best of wishes. Prithee, tell me
    What trick didst **thou** invent to come to Rome
    Without **thy** husband?
JULIA:
                Why, my lord, I told him
    I came to visit an old anchorite
    Here for devotion.
CARDINAL:
              Thou art a witty false one,
    I mean, to him.
JULIA:
              You have prevail'd with me
    Beyond my strongest thoughts: I would not now
    Find **you** inconstant.
CARDINAL:
              Do not put **thyself**
    To such a voluntary torture, which proceeds
    Out of **your** own guilt.

JULIA:
  How, my lord?
CARDINAL:
              You fear
  My constancy, because you have approv'd
  Those giddy and wild turnings in **yourself.**

One impulse many script editors have is to normalize every "thou" to "you." Modern audiences rarely hear "thou," and they are likely to think it is formal rather than informal. However, these distinctions offer so much information and clarity to actors, we argue for leaving them as they are. This scene is less dynamic if we lose the sense of instability in this relationship, which the Cardinal creates through lines like "Do not put **thyself** / To such a voluntary torture, which proceeds / Out of **your** own guilt." As you cut scenes with multiple second-person pronouns, be careful not to accidentally eliminate patterns. It's *important* the Cardinal uses both types of pronouns in this scene. A cut which ends this beat of the scene after "Do not put thyself to such a voluntary torture," would miss the moment where the Cardinal harshly distances himself from Julia. The end of the play (where he kills her by making her kiss a poisoned Bible, because that's how Webster does things) makes much less sense if we've only ever seen the Cardinal be genuinely intimate with Julia.

Fingerprints

Some playwrights have hallmark rhetorical patterns they can be identified by. John Marston, for example, was the butt of his contemporaries' jokes for his insistence on florid language, and never used a plain word when a fancy one was available. Marston peppered his play *Antonio's Revenge* with sentences like: "Then, death, like to a stifling incubus, / Lie on my bosom. Lo, see, I am sped. / My breast is Golgotha, grave for the dead," Ben Jonson found Marston's language so objectionable he wrote a play wherein Marston's thinly veiled avatar has to vomit up his fancy words (including "incubus").

Others were famous for the specifics of their verse. Ben Jonson praised Christopher Marlowe's "mighty line," for the way his iambic pentameter bangs along with minimal, if any, deviation: "Was **this** the **face** that **launched** a **thou**sand **ships**?" As we've already discussed, Webster, on the other hand, has piles of irregularities in his rhythms.

George Bernard Shaw can be a challenge to cut because one of his hallmarks is his over-the-top language. As Martine Kei Green-Rogers noted,

> part of the decadent world that Shaw creates is about the fact that people can languish in language. To me, part of getting into the weeds with Shaw is about how to honor the voice while also doing what needs to be done in terms of getting it shorter… Even with the cuts, how do I still allow that to happen?

Some playwrights are notable for themes or patterns of ideas which are part of the fabric of their oeuvre. Shakespeare fills his plays with ambiguity and contradiction. While it might seem helpful to simplify or "correct" his ambiguities through cuts (to make *A Midsummer Night's Dream* take exactly one night, for example, or to untangle whether Cassio actually *did* have the opportunity to sleep with Desdemona), these ambiguities are a big part of what makes Shakespeare's plays compelling.

Some periods of drama prioritized spectacle over character or humor over plot. Cuts require you to understand what your modern audience wants in a theatrical event, and the framework of the play's era. If you find yourself knotted up in some details which don't make sense, take a step back and look at the play's context. Fight your own assumptions about what a play should be. As Antoni Cimolino told us,

> A wise man once said: 'Who is so smart as to understand the plot of a Restoration comedy? And who is so stupid as to care?' When you take a great Restoration playwright, especially [William] Congreve, by the time you remove all of the non-narrative, there's *no reason to do the play*. It is only in his reflections upon life and humanity, and the beautiful turns of phrase—those are the things you're actually watching the play for, and they're the very things you *can* cut.

Know what the play wants to be before you try to change it.

Each playwright has a precise combination of verse pattern, diction, line length, and distribution of lines which act as a fingerprint for their work. Full analysis of these details is the work of computers and people with plenty of time on their hands, but through some consideration to each of these aspects and how the playwright at hand employs them, we can create cuts that still *feel*, at a gut level, like they belong to a particular playwright.

As just one example, Centlivre, in a play nearly all in prose, tacks on poems as a button on some of her scenes. Here are two examples of this device:

COLONEL FAINWELL:

> Bold was the Man who ventur'd first to Sea,
> But the first vent'ring Lovers bolder were:
> The Path of Love's a dark and dangerous Way,
> Without a Landmark, or one friendly Star,
> And he that runs the Risque, deserves the Fair.

LOVELY:

> O all ye Powers, that favour happy Lovers, grant he may be mine! Thou God of Love, if thou be'st ought but Name, assist my Fainwell.
> Point all thy Darts to aid my Love's Design,
> And make his Plots as prevalent as thine.

Each gives the scene a sense of completion. They also give the audience an instant of alone time with the character, an insight into their private thoughts. Some measure of the play's charm rests in these moments of connection. Without them, it would be less entertaining, less conspiratorial, and, crucially, less *Centlivre*. This isn't to say they are entirely uncuttable, but just that you should think twice.

Cut it! But with care

We have spent a lot of time on the reasons playwrights include particular types of language in their work. Playwrights knew their business, and you should trust them. With that said, this is a book about cuts. We think plays *should* be cut, for the specific context of your production. We get irritated with plays presented uncut when they should be trimmed, and with plays cut haphazardly. Understand what you cut, and justify what you include and remove.

7 Cut to the Moment
Production-Specific Cuts

Very rarely are cuts universal. A cut which might work beautifully in an outdoor venue for a touring company might be entirely lost when housed at a cavernous indoor space, performed by a large ensemble. An effective four-hour cut at a big-city arts festival might be beyond the abilities of your high school drama club. Every cut should respond to the production it serves. You can find cuts (particularly of early modern plays) on the internet, but these are cut in a generic sense, to offer a starting point. None of these cuts takes into account the needs of *your* director, *your* audience, *your* venue. And this, of course, is the reason this book exists at all: to help you cut *your* play for *your* production.

Additionally—and this is a somewhat grey area—if you adopt another artist's cut, you need to be aware of intellectual property limitations (for more, see Appendix 1). Say, for example, you watch the Royal National Theatre's streamed NTLive version of Racine's *Phèdre* (1677) on YouTube. And say you illegally download the YouTube video and manually copy the text cut for yourself. If you use this cut exactly as-is, it can be problematic. While it is difficult to prove a cut has been re-used for another production, be aware that most cuts are production-specific, and have been tailored through rehearsal and performance to fit to a company, space, and directorial vision. By all means, if you notice a bold dramaturgical choice which inspires, the nature of public performance is that it may be adopted or expanded upon. But that's the grey area. Inspiration is one thing, but a straight-up copy of textual cuts isn't advisable. Why? Beyond the legal questions, it's this: it's not your production, so the cuts don't respond to your specific production variables.

Production variables: concept and context

Let's say you're in an established festival space with a set group of repertory actors, and you want to produce *The Cherry Orchard* (1903). Why not dust off the same version you produced six years ago? For starters: what's changed in six years? In the words of Heraclitus, "No man ever steps in the same river twice, for it's not the same river and he's not the same man." You likely have a different cast, perhaps a different director, and almost certainly a different

DOI: 10.4324/9781003160076-8

concept. The world has changed. Audiences have changed. Politically. Technologically. Ideologically. To ignore those changes is to risk "museum theatre." No one wants museum theatre.

Indeed, production variables are a factor for even the most prolific of cutters. James Shapiro, who has cut half of Shakespeare's canon, begins *every* cut with a sit-down with the play's director to go through the play, line by line. For Shapiro, the first cut is "a basis for the conversation," and for the first two to three weeks of preproduction it's a "negotiated text." Then, the play changes further in rehearsal, to make adjustments for one particular cast and particular concept. Dusting off someone else's cut and trying to mold a concept to it ultimately creates *more* work in the long run, not less.

The other reason not to stick with an old cut? Your audience. They, almost certainly, are different from the group who approved of a cut six years ago. We don't mean the actual people—you may have a loyal subscriber base who returns year after year—but your audience's context based on what has happened in the world over the last six years. In the published screenplay for *Richard III*, Ian McKellen tells an instructive tale of Richard Eyre's 1989 stage production at the Royal National Theatre. This production notably set Gloucester as a blackshirted Nazi figure, replaced swastikas on red banners with an ugly boar's head, and costumed Richard's followers as the Gestapo. Staged in London, this was a popular production which set the charismatic antihero as the common enemy of all Britons: Hitler. When the production toured, however, there was a varied response around Europe:

> Audiences across the world took the point [of the play's design] and revealed a paradox: the more specific a production, the more general its relevance. Although our story was obviously an English one, audiences took the message personally wherever we toured. In Hamburg, Richard's blackshirt troops seemed like a commentary on the Third Reich. In Bucharest, when Richard was slain, the Romanians stopped the show with heartfelt cheers, in memory of their recent freedom from Ceausescu's regime. In Cairo, as the Gulf War was hotting up, it all seemed like a new play about Saddam Hussein. (13)

The point here is that the audience brought their own context to the table: to assume your 2009 cut of a script will hold up in a post-Trump, post-COVID world is short-sighted. A fresh cut will fit your moment. As Shapiro notes, the challenge a cutter comes up against is "How do you do a cut without imposing your vision of the play on the director? That is crucial." If you attend the first sit-down with a director with a dusted-off copy of an old cut, that's exactly what you're doing: imposing your vision.

A specific production is the confluence of many factors. Some, like the audience and the space, we have discussed in other chapters. Others include:

- Casting (size, gender, race, age, experience)
- Concept

- Venue (or, for a touring show, venues)
- Touring
- Design
- Virtual Logistics

Each piece creates the unique experience of a production. Even when the design is similar to another show's or the core group of actors have worked together for a decade, each production is unique. The magic of theatre is its ability—its *requirement*—to be different every night. An engaged audience bends the shape of the story. A morning headline changes how the matinee's words land. One actor makes a discovery in the moment and the whole cast responds with harmonic resonance. Tune your cut to the distinct conditions of your production, and you create support for its particular magic.

Casting—size, gender, race, age, experience

Some words which call attention to the actor's body can enhance the production. If your first impulse is to take them out, question it. Sometimes, the juxtaposition between *actor* and *character* can change the way the audience hears the text. One discovery audience members consistently report on seeing plays with cross-gendered casting is that gendered words *pop* in their ears. They hear them in a new way. These reactions can be deep-seated: when a Black actor plays a character where he either has to call someone else a slave or be called a slave, those words land differently than when both people in the dialog are white. "Slave" was a much less loaded word in the early modern period than it is today, particularly to a modern North American audience. In 16th-century England, it meant a person of low status, often a servant,

---

Grant Mudge:
I think we're supposed to look at Lysander in a negative way when we hear him say, "Out, tawny Tartar, out!" and "Away, you Ethiope." We left "tawny Tartar," but "Ethiope" chafed us. Cameron Knight was playing Lysander [and several other roles]. He came up to me and he said, "Can we talk about 'Ethiope'?"

I said, "Absolutely. I can't figure out what to do with that. I think we have to cut it."

He said, "Well, I had an idea. Do you know the word 'heliotrope'?"
"That's brilliant!" I told him.

It's a clinging vine. It preserved the same kind of sound. It was derogatory—it's kind of a weed—and it was doing exactly what Hermia was doing—I'll cling to thee!

7.1 Excerpt from interview with Grant Mudge, 22 January 2021.

but did not necessarily imply ownership. The word "slave" appears dozens of times in the works of Ben Jonson. It is used six times each in both *Every Man Out Of His Humour* and *Sejanus His Fall* (1603) as a derogatory descriptive word: "You most notorious whelp, you insolent slave" "Slave, I could bite thine ear." "Where is he? Which is he? He is a slave!" "What, rogues, bawds, slaves, you'll open the door." Each instance describes a person of lower status, without the baggage the term carries today, but your audience won't hear it the way Jonson's audience did.

When 21st-century audiences hear that word spoken by one white person to another, they generally understand the usage is antiquated, but crucially, they hear it in a very modern—and uncomfortable—way when a Black actor plays the low-status character.

Should we cut language which makes our audiences uncomfortable? It depends. Sometimes, we *want* our audience to be uncomfortable, or to use discomfort to enhance our storytelling. In her brilliant document, "Dismantling Anti-Black Linguistic Racism in Shakespeare," Lavina Jadhwani argues the definition of "slave" defies casual usage. The word

> has changed too much for us to now use it in the original context. As an American audience member, it's challenging to hear this word and not think of the history of slavery in the United States and the transgenerational trauma that Black people experience today. The altered meaning will alter the stakes of the moment.

This last point is crucial; we must be aware of how these changed valences affect how an audience and actors hear words. Your decision to cut or change the word depends on how you want the audience to feel about the people who say it and the people who receive it. If a Black actor plays a servant, the audience may judge the person who calls him a "slave" more harshly than the playwright originally intended. If this is the story we want to tell, we should allow "slave" to stand. If it's not, we should cut or replace it. Jadhwani suggests substitution: "knave" is close to an early modern sense, and conveniently rhymes and scans.

Sometimes a minor cut can defuse a line which time has rendered problematic. Tim Carroll offered this example from *Charley's Aunt* (1892), where Sir Frances informs his son Jack he's found a job for the young man. In Bengal. Jack's response is, "Bengal? What a horrible place!" "It's one of those things," Carroll said,

> where you think, 'That's just going to bump people out of the play,' and all you need to know is that he doesn't want to go and move to the other side of the world for his first job. It doesn't matter where it is. So all I did was cut the 'What a horrible place.' It's all perfectly contained in 'Bengal?'

While our job as artists is to occasionally offer constructive discomfort, we should *never* extend it to making our collaborators feel *unsafe*. Some language,

Kate Mulvany:
Design comes into it so, so much. Even lighting. It's just so important for me as an adapter, a cutter, to also find out what people's favorite moments are as well. It is not just the design team in a way that I'm working around. It's the actors themselves. For some actors, some things that might not feel interesting to me, might in another way, culturally or gender-wise, sexuality-wise, be really important to another actor to say it. So I'm always fascinated by that, something that I might not be able to bring much meaning to as an actor will be completely different in someone else's hands. So I really like to check in on the team before I cut anything really important, but I'll often get in touch with the cast before I even start the adaptation process or the cutting process to say 'What are your favorite bits? What are your babies that you just don't want to throw out with the bathwater?' and I think that's a really respectful way as well of getting the team together.

7.2 Excerpt from interview with Kate Mulvany, 14 February 2021.

especially that which is racially charged or misogynist, can be traumatic for actors to say and to hear, night after night. Engage in conversation with people who will have to say and hear these difficult words. Leave the words in only with the performers' informed consent. If your role allows, check in again halfway through the rehearsal process, and have an honest conversation where removal is still on the table. Your vision for the play is much less important than actors' safety, in every dimension—physical, spiritual, and emotional.

A production may re-gender a character: that is, to not only have the *actor* be of a different gender than the character, but to change the *character's* gender. This approach can update an old play for a modern audience. Imagine how *The Seagull* would change if Konstantin were played as a woman. The Masha/Konstantin/Nina triangle would suddenly have new dimensions, as would Konstantin's relationship with Irina. But take care to think about how this choice impacts the script and the story. When a play's text intersects with an actor's body, you may want to cut it, or not. But don't ignore it.

Keep in mind, also, the age and experience of your actors. With very young actors, some of the play's bawdy jokes may need to go. For the inexperienced, an ensemble cut, focused on evenly distributing lines, can make the process easier for everyone by spreading the work around.

Microcast cuts—or a cut which boils down the play to a manageable size for a cast of three or four actors—can be a particular challenge. These can, however, be extremely rewarding, especially for audiences with a short attention span. To perform any classical play with a cast of three or four inevitably changes the fundamental makeup of the play, and requires extensive doubling and omission of major characters and stories.

Scott Kaiser, long of the Oregon Shakespeare Festival, mastered the microcast when he collaborated with a group of like-minded actors to develop 40-minute versions of Shakespeare's plays for the OSF School Visit Program. To prepare these truncated texts, Kaiser used keys very similar to our Three Questions. He recommends film-like storyboards to visualize and understand where your characters will be and what they need, to focus on the key actions for each play (Kaiser 8–9).

Microcasts mean losses are unavoidable: much of the original texture depends on character interaction and lively crowd scenes. Madcap doubling with different hats at breakneck speed is an absolutely valuable adaptation exercise, but it's impossible to maintain *every* element of the original. A microcast is a cost-efficient way to tour a play, and to highlight selected themes and concepts. It is, however, ultimately a process of narrative simplification. The microcast cut process is essentially identical to a cut for a larger cast, but with an even tighter focus and greater willingness to let a lot of the play go. There are many excellent resources available which present small-cast, shortened Shakespeare, such as Kaiser's *Have Shakespeare Will Travel*, and Julie Fain Lawrence-Edsell's *One Hour Shakespeare* series which present microcast cuts. We enthusiastically recommend both as starting points.

Concept

The idea of "concept" can be a prickly one. When directors don't trust the text to do the work for them, they tend to lean heavily on their concept. Concepts have their uses; a bold concept may illuminate an obscure and outdated text. An exploration of *A Game at Chess* (1624) that explicitly comments on its connections to a present political situation may connect with an audience at a deep level, where a straight-down-the-middle take is nearly guaranteed to leave them bored or bewildered. All productions have some sort of concept, whether or not the director chooses to use the term. Some concepts have a light hand, and might be better understood as a lens for examining the play. Others are in your face, impossible to ignore. Both have implications.

The director's concept may be different from your idea for the play. We return to James Shapiro's description of the conversation that precedes every cut, which is vital for you to understand what play the director hopes for. While you can offer your perspective, remember it is the director's play and you should cut to their vision. *The Wild Duck* (1894) set on an aircraft carrier? Okay. *Lucius Junius Brutus* (1681) in the aftermath of the Capitol Riots? Sure. *Dulcitius* (c.935) set in Hrosvitha's Abbey of Gandersheim? Great. These concepts (of varied playability) are the frame in which you cut. To get a better sense of how this use of concept works, see our selection of approaches to *Richard III* below.

Venue

One of the best things about theatre is its specificity. Unlike a film—performed exactly the same way in every venue, for every audience, in every decade—a play responds to its context. One of the most powerful pieces of context is the *venue*. If your production is indoors, some lines land differently than if it is outdoors. If the venue uses universal lighting, where the actors can see the audience, some lines resound with more clarity than if they're in the dark. Your cuts should be attentive to the venue.

Venues have a specific stage architecture, which in itself tells the audience what to expect from the performance. Your cut must take this into account. Consider each of these architectural factors and ask yourself whether they will necessarily influence your cut.

- Immediately outside:
  - Did the audience enter through a massive lobby with crystal chandeliers and plush carpets?
  - Did they shuffle down to the cafetorium from third period?

7.3 At the American Shakespeare Center's Blackfriars Theater, audiences and actors share light and make eye contact.

- Were they on an after-dinner walk when they noticed your lighting rig in the park?
- The framing of the stage:
  - Is there a proscenium to create a fourth wall between your audience and actors?
  - Is the audience seated on a sharp rake above your stage?
  - Is the house large enough that those in the cheap seats brought binoculars, or small enough the furthest seat is within a three-point shot of the stage?
  - Are there specific elements of the stage architecture your set cannot or will not change, like on-stage balconies, entrances through the audience, or permanent doors?
- The relationship between actors and audience:
  - Is the goal of the performance to *create an illusion* or to *present a story*?
  - Can your actors and audience see each other?
  - Can the audience members see each other?
  - Are your actors and audience encouraged to interact?

Certain periods of drama were more metatheatrical than others. The Elizabethans constantly referred to the spaces in which they played, where the Naturalists of the 19th century deliberately ignored it. Your theatre may have physical features the playwright would not have expected, or lack ones common in their theatre. Your cut should respond to these differences. In *Englishmen for My Money* (1598), William Haughton has a character warn his scene partner: "Take heed, sir, here's a post." Haughton's players worked in a theatre where large posts held up the balcony; he incorporated the architecture of the theatre into his character's words. If your theatre is not similarly equipped, your set designer might thank you for a sensitive edit.

The size of your venue will affect your cut, as well. Both Lue Douthit (Oregon Shakespeare Festival) and Antoni Cimolino (Stratford Festival, Canada) gave logistical answers to questions about different cuts in different venues. Both noted an entrance on one of the theater's larger stages would be far different from one on a studio or black box stage. Cimolino told us,

> Getting to centre stage at the [Tom] Patterson [Theatre, a long alley stage], as [former Artistic Director] Richard Monette would say, 'You have to pack a lunch.' And so the timing can change… Immediate entrances become a little bit longer and so you allow for some of that travel time, which I know sounds finicky, but you just realize there's no point trying to cut that: you're going to have dead air.

If an actor needs some lead-time to make it to center stage, it's worthwhile padding the text to let them get there.

7.4 The Tom Patterson Theatre at the Stratford Festival (shown here in its newly renovated 2021 state) features an alley stage which makes entrances a major consideration.

Some venues have rules and restrictions about performances in their spaces. If you take a play into a middle school, the administration might expect you to play down any particularly raunchy bits. Many prison performance programs face restrictions on anything which remotely resembles a weapon (even water guns). They have to adapt their texts to avoid references to swords or daggers, or develop a stylized portrayal of violence.

Venues also differ in the relationship—both physical and emotional—between the actor and the audience. Consider the theatrical convention of the aside. In pre-electric theatres, if an actor had an aside, they would speak directly to the audience, which they could see as clearly as their scene partners. In a theatrical arrangement where the audience is invisible and unacknowledged, an aside can distract and feel unnatural. As Jeremy Lopez suggests, asides "impinge on an audience's focus to a certain degree" (57) as they remind them they are at a play. However, if the context allows the actor to connect directly with the audience, to speak as one human to another, it can enhance the play, draw them in, and encourage them to ally with the character. If your space and performance style doesn't allow the actor to acknowledge the existence of the audience, consider limited asides. Be aware that sometimes, audience members respond to questions characters ask them.

We once saw a memorable student matinee of *The Taming of the Shrew,* in a venue where the audience and actors shared light. In response to Petruchio's line, "He that knows better how to tame a shrew, / Now let him speak; 'tis charity to shew," a high schooler shouted, "Smack the bitch!" Although the actor responded with aplomb, given the venue and audience, this line might have been less distracting if it were removed.

If your performances are outdoors, try not to cut lines about the natural world. Ones not relevant to your current conditions will slide past your audience's ear, but if you catch a rainy day in your run of *Dido, Queen of Carthage* (1593), the crowd will howl with delight at the line, "Did ever men see such a sudden storm? / Or day so clear so suddenly o'er cast?" British actor Anna Northam shared a story about her Helena in an outdoor production of *A Midsummer Night's Dream,* on a stage surrounded by overhanging trees. She was halfway through the "Oh, I am out of breath in this fond chase" speech, when suddenly:

> There was a crash in the trees. I didn't look up, but the audience was now distracted. I just thought, 'I'm going to keep going,' and then suddenly, right by me—it nearly took my ear off—a squirrel fell out of the trees, literally brushing me. It fell straight onto the stage. The audience gasped. I just froze, and looked down, and it was motionless on the ground. I thought, 'Oh crap, it's dead! That's going to ruin my speech… and also, oh, my God, the poor thing!' So, I went up to it, really slowly, and it got up, looked at me for about three seconds—we were sort of eyeballing each other—and then it just ran off. I thought, 'Oh, thank God!' The audience sighed. I thought, 'Where am I, in the speech?' I was just before those lines: 'No, no, I am as ugly as a bear, for beasts that meet me run away for fear!' That was my next line. It was fortuitous timing. Of course, I milked it for everything, and got a standing ovation.

If that line had been cut, it would have been a massive missed opportunity.

Touring

It may seem like an obvious statement, but a play on tour is different from a play at home. We're surprised at how often textual adjustment is shunted to one side when a company chooses to take their work on the road. In many ways it's logical: after an initial, successful run, to cut the script for the purposes of a tour might feel risky. Chances are, however, your set and lights change on the road, simplified to fit to any space, so why not your text? Whether your production travels on the strength of your success (good for you!) or if it was conceived as a touring production, the ability to fit into any space is crucial.

Even back in Elizabethan England, touring considerations were a priority for companies: a play which worked well in the playhouse in London also had to work on the back of a wagon in Lincolnshire. What do those audiences need? We can see from the various states of individually printed texts in the late 16th and early 17th centuries that words shifted and changed, for which touring logistics were likely responsible. Perhaps they adjusted the run time, with a less patient, more transient audience. Or removed those local references which really killed at home.

For a tour, think about whether your cut would hold up away from your local patrons. Will this appeal to people from all walks of life? All levels of experience and education? Sometimes a deft cut will save you the chore of a slog through a text-heavy explication scene which won't land on tour. Flexibility is the goal, particularly if your text is reliant on physical spaces you might not have available to you in all venues.

Design

Design might seem like an unusual consideration as you cut, but if you neglect the work on the design side, you run the risk of a script that is out of sync with its environment. Kate Mulvany discussed the importance of design when it comes to her cuts. On one project, developed in association with Australia's Yirra Yaakin Theatre Company and Bell Shakespeare, Kate worked as dramaturg for Indigenous Australian adapter Kylie Bracknell (Kaarljilba Kaardn) as Kylie adapted *Macbeth* into the West Australian Noongar dialect. Kylie was immediately drawn to the minor character of Hecate,

7.5 The stunning world of *Hecate* focused on a character nearly always cut.

who appears only briefly, in a scene widely believed not to have been written by Shakespeare. When Kylie discovered Hecate was often cut, she pushed back: "Why would you cut the 'Boss Lady' of the Weïrd Sisters?" Not only was Hecate left entirely uncut, but the Noongar-language production revolved around her—and was even entitled *Hecate*. This informed the physical design and dramaturgical process.

James Shapiro discussed with us the highly successful Public Works project, which presents Shakespeare with a community-based cast, interlaced with music and song. When he cut *Twelfth Night*, not only did he have to take into account a community performer soundscape, but he had to cut the text itself down to only 1,000 lines to accommodate the additional production design.

Particularly in plays from periods where imagination was more important than illusion—the Ancient Greeks, the Elizabethan English, the Spanish Siglo de Oro, among others—the playwrights' words create the "design" of the play. If you approach a play from one of these periods in a theatre with a big design budget, consider descriptive language an opportunity to cut. If your design team will create an intense shipwrecking storm, you can probably cut the language Jonson, Chapman, and Marston use for the same purpose in *Eastward, Ho!* (1605). Don't completely give way though. The shipwreck from *The Tempest* might be beautifully and technologically rendered through design, but without the plaintive cries of sailors and nobles alike, the scene just isn't the same.

Virtual logistics

As we wrote this book in the midst of the global COVID-19 pandemic of the early 2020s, we were aware we invited the risk of immediately dated contemporary references. The rise and immediate ubiquity of virtual performance is, however, an innovation which may be here to stay.

Throughout the pandemic lockdowns, faced with ballooning financial shortfalls, subscriber bases desperate for substitute entertainment in pandemic lockdowns, and shuttered physical theatre spaces, theater companies pivoted into the potential of virtual theatre. What began as YouTube releases of past archival videos and cinematic releases (by companies such as the Royal National Theatre, the Royal Shakespeare Company, and the Stratford Festival, Canada), moved quickly toward custom-created virtual performances. Performances grew and flourished on platforms such as ZOOM, YouTube, and Vimeo, and new technology rushed to fill the void for companies who looked to innovate.

With innovation, of course, came limitations. As companies sought to create virtual-specific works, it was clear stage-dependent scripts did not function in the same way when actors were not present in the same space. Companies had to adapt to the new environment, which included consideration of how texts would be handled. But how do you cut for a ZOOM performance? What is necessary? Is it different? In what ways?

It's not greatly different from any other type of cut: return to the Three Questions, and add your virtual constraints to the list. Incorporate the logistics of play cuts for virtual performance as just another mode of expression, with an eye to how this might differ from a live event. While most audience members would prefer to watch plays in a live environment, companies have identified virtual performance as an intriguing new aspect to their cultural suite, and even after pandemic lockdowns eased, virtual performance could remain a normal element of theatrical presentation.

Virtual stages are stages nonetheless, and any adapter who assumes the rules of the virtual performance are essentially the same as the rules of the live theatre is reckless at worst, and ignorant of the possibilities at best. Virtual theatre offers technologically based innovations often too expensive to attempt in a live theatre: a virtual Ariel who flits about the sails of Alonzo's ship was a mammoth spectacular when achieved by Gregory Doran in his 2017 RSC *The Tempest*, underwritten by software giant Intel, but on the virtual screen, such an effect is a much simpler (albeit less impressive!) proposition. You should take the environment into account as you cut and change texts. The virtual environment is as much a priority as a specific physical space.

The first place any virtual cut begins is again in the directorial concept, which determines how the medium is used. Is the video window (on whatever platform you use) part of the world of the play or do the actors ignore it? So, in your virtual *Machinal*, is Helen depicted as "in the room" with the machinery of her life or does your directorial concept build on the experience of isolation in front of a computer screen? Do your actors acknowledge the medium or ignore it and pretend they are still in a theatre? Does your design mimic a theatre experience with green-screen and actors superimposed together in a single frame? Are there virtual backgrounds? Or do we see the actor's bed behind them, while they perform from a desk chair?

Virtual performance adds a complicated, often unwelcome, layer to the dramaturgical mix. Audiences untangle meaning as boxed-in characters speak earnestly into a web-camera, perhaps surrounded by a shimmering, uncanny valley of virtual background. Even as audiences accept this reality, text cuts that assume a physical theatre space miss the medium's possibilities.

The possibilities of virtual performance include features prohibitively expensive in the physical theatre space. In a very short time, virtual performance has evolved from static cameras and individual cubes which display each actor's personal apartment, to something far closer to television editing, with coordinated camera focus, costumes, props, and superimposed video. Companies experiment with chat functions and JamBoards to connect with audiences, and over the course of lockdown, have revolved textual cuts around smaller casts, focused narratives, and expedient story.

Why do we need a specific cut for virtual audiences? Any performance outside of the streamlined focus provided by a physical theatre space should take the audience's experience into account. It is not hyperbolic to suggest that virtual theatre is performed for the most distracted theatre audiences of the last 200 years, or perhaps ever. From the comfort of home, on a television, computer, or even cell-phone, virtual audiences are more prone than ever to multitask or half-listen. Distractions are no longer Elizabethan orange-sellers and pickpockets or see-and-be-seen Restoration posturing. Online performers vie with the accessible lure of the internet, only an idle click away. If a play is too long, too speechy, too unvaried, the anonymous device-addicted audience member can happily scroll Facebook throughout an entire performance and not disturb performers or other patrons. Add the actors' challenge of how to perform without the energy of an audience and the proximity of other artists, and virtual theatre can be a slog. Expedient, clear cuts which lean toward dialogue and minimize soliloquy help maintain audience and actor focus.

A text heavy on untethered pronouns is an extreme challenge, as tracking antecedents is nearly impossible. Script edits may go beyond the typical removal of extraneous detail, and include extra repetition of character names for clarity. Scripts heavy on physical movement provide a special challenge. Say, for example, you stage a virtual *Much Ado About Nothing*, which features two comic eavesdropping scenes. As Benedick and then Beatrice "hide" on screen, many subtle details possible on the physical stage are lost, which will impact your cut. Shakespeare's tendency to over-describe can be (as we have discussed) a rich area for text cuts, to allow actors to show rather than tell. In a virtual environment, such text is far more important. A line which simply describes action ("So angle we for Beatrice; who even now / Is couched in the woodbine coverture.") shifts from an easy excision for physical performance, to vital context for a virtual audience's imagination.

A virtual cut removes the onus from the corporeal presence and brings focus back to the verbal storytelling, in a manner aligned to radio drama. The immense *reach* of virtual performance is another commonality with radio. With a mere click of a link and a small access fee, audiences from around the world can tune in to virtual performances in a manner not possible in physical spaces. Never before has the performance world been so small, where a theatre lover can watch Chekhov in Moscow, Molière in Paris, and Soyinka in Johannesburg on the same day. Recorded performance is not new, but the liveness and community of virtual performance means reach is limited only by a stable internet connection. While exciting, this also includes caveats: one director we spoke to discussed a virtual performance of *Machinal* minutely (and with permission) adjusted to remove racial slurs from several select moments. The limitless reach of the virtual environment made this necessary. In a physical theatre space, such words—palatable in 1928 but problematic today—could be contextualized and discussed to ensure the audience was clear on the justifications for its presence. On the internet (and particularly at the height of the Black Lives Matter movement, which coincided with this production), it is extremely easy for audiences to take statements out of context, or even to edit the video, maliciously misrepresenting the work.

Case study: *Richard III* in production

To highlight the ways cuts respond to a variety of productions, we want to examine several productions of the same play. As it happens, both of us, as well as nearly everyone we interviewed, has worked on Shakespeare's *Richard III*. As we compare a selection of various real productions, we can examine how cuts support the concept or conditions of a production. The more we explore these cuts, the more we discover the infinite variety contained in this one play text.

Productions of *Richard III* necessarily respond to and comment on the actors' bodies, particularly because Shakespeare so clearly describes Richard's body. Famously—perhaps infamously—Shakespeare emphasizes Richard's twisted spine, with references to his scoliosis manifested as "bunch-back'd," with a withered arm like a "blasted sapling," in a physical condition so appalling, "sent into this world half made up," that "dogs bark at [him] as [he] halts by them." Historically true or not, this is an evocative charge for any actor, and by extension, text cutter.

As a case in point, Kate Mulvany spoke at length about her acclaimed *Richard 3*, which she adapted for Bell Shakespeare (Australia), and in which she appeared as the titular king. This text had a particular significance for her: not only is she a direct descendant of the historical Richard III, but as the result of a childhood cancer, she has the same physical spinal disability as her character. She was forced to ask the often-unasked question: "When you have a disabled actor, how do you cut the play around them?" In this production, they cut the script to emphasize the connection between her real body and Richard's, investing in those descriptions where other productions might elide them. What's more, she played Richard as a man, but at a memorable point, revealed her spine—and her breasts—to emphasize her physical resemblance to the historical Richard, with an added layer. This character was so far twisted he had somehow become a woman. This was an incredibly rare confluence of circumstances to elevate the play with a new commentary.

Another decision is how you will manage the politics of *Richard III* and its connection to the present day. For example, Toby adapted the play for an essentially unrecognizable university production, re-titled *#R3* (2013, directed by Jennifer Roberts-Smith).

This adaptation focused on a concept of surveillance, social media, and direct address: a digital world inspired by Jeremy Bentham's Panopticon. In this production, all efforts were made to over-emphasize direct address, and Toby's cut was informed by supplementary design elements that incorporated

112 *Cut to the Moment: Production-Specific Cuts*

7.6 Kate Mulvany's striking *Richard 3* explored unexpected avenues in the character.

social media posts and live camera with text on screen. The directive that drove the concept was to remove anything which could not be communicated through direct address of some sort, be it through aside, soliloquy, or social media reportage (which is in itself direct address to users). The first stage direction notes:

Some notes on the rules of the world:
 Two spaces: the broadcast centre and the conceptual "space" of the Internet. The audience and the Citizens are in the broadcast centre. Communication devices are as powerful as weapons. Bodily contact is rare and reserved for violence. Richard is at the centre; the world revolves around him.

In this world, Richard's victims not only appealed to the audience for their support but also reached out through social media channels, with Twitter feeds and Facebook posts to resist Richard's rise to power; Richmond's final invasion was achieved in a "hack" of Richard's digital redoubt. The challenge was to reduce the interior world with no place in this production, and to heighten what was externalized and public. The result was a 75-minute cut of a famously long play, with frequent substitution of social media shorthand to replace lengthy scenes. This included a mash-up viral video of soundbites that played as a Trojan Horse virus uploaded to Richard's command center, in place of Richard's pre-battle nightmare. It also used the now-familiar videochat

7.7 Kandi Prosser (Lady Anne Neville), Leah Magdalen (Queen Elizabeth), and Meghan Jones (The Duchess of York) offer their curses to Richard's security camera outside The Tower as Catesby (Jessica Blondin) and Brakenbury (Erik Johnson) look on.

screens as effective entrances and exits: "messengers" were replaced by text messages; Buckingham infers the bastardy of Richard's nephews in a Tweet.

The result? An experiment which tested the limits of public communication within the world of *Richard III*. Citizens showed their support in viral Retweets. Even the title, a bare-bones hashtag, demonstrated this was not Shakespeare's *Richard III* anymore, but was designed to speak to the modern students on campus. Lines from the citizenry were converted to a projected social media stream scroll across the cyclorama. Live camera feeds meant characters could interrupt and interject, and used the mute function to allow for a clever approach to asides, boldly in front of oblivious victims. In this environment, the concept meant the text cut shaped to what was presented.

Many Shakespeare companies experiment with cross-gendered casting. Gender politics are at the crux of *Richard III*, making it rich with opportunity. In Jenny Bennett's 2018 production of *Richard III* at the American Shakespeare Center (Staunton, VA), John Harrell played Richard's mother, the Duchess of York. Although Harrell's costume was a dress and clearly intended to read as female, he wasn't in drag. Audience members understood that a male actor represented a female character. A director who expected less of her audience might have cut the Duchess' many references to her womb ("O my accursed womb, the bed of death!") when she knew the words would be spoken by an actor who clearly did not have a uterus. Bennett let those words stand, granting the lines an unusual power, at least in part because they played against the audience's expectations.

In Aili's award-winning 2019 production at the Pigeon Creek Shakespeare Company (Grand Rapids, MI) a female actor played the First Murderer, and the Duke of Clarence was played by a nonbinary actor whom audiences typically read as female. One moment of unusual power came when the First Murderer refused Clarence's demand that he abandon his murderous mission with, "Relent! 'tis cowardly and womanish." Both the speaker and the recipient of the misogynist language had real-life experience with it. The Murderer knew how it felt to be treated as weak because of her gender, and so did the Duke. Their mutual, bone-deep sense of that word's power gave it more weight than it would have had if both actors had been men.

To the extent that Aili's production had a concept, it was, "Mothers and Sons." When she read the play to prepare her cut, she realized that, although she had seen several productions of it, she had never seen the full extent of the women's power. Many productions minimize women, cut Lady Anne except for the famous seduction scene, and conflate Queen Margaret and the Duchess of York, which diminishes both of their power. In Shakespeare's text, grieving mothers drive the action. Margaret, near-mad with grief, lays a curse in Act One, Scene Two, to set the whole story in motion:

> Can curses pierce the clouds and enter heaven?
> Why, then, give way, dull clouds, to my quick curses!
> If not by war, by surfeit die your king,
> As ours by murder, to make him a king!
> Edward thy son, which now is Prince of Wales,
> For Edward my son, which was Prince of Wales,
> Die in his youth by like untimely violence!
> Thyself a queen, for me that was a queen,
> Outlive thy glory, like my wretched self!
> Long mayst thou live to wail thy children's loss;
> And see another, as I see thee now,
> Deck'd in thy rights, as thou art stall'd in mine!

Lady Anne curses Richard as she mourns her father-in-law:

> Cursed be the hand that made these fatal holes!
> Cursed be the heart that had the heart to do it!
> Cursed the blood that let this blood from hence!

Queen Elizabeth, who has lost a husband and four sons, begs Margaret to teach her to curse.

> O thou well skill'd in curses, stay awhile,
> And teach me how to curse mine enemies!

7.8 Margaret (Kate Bode) torments Queen Elizabeth (Katherine Mayberry) in Pigeon Creek Shakespeare's *Richard III*.

In this play, women mourn their children, over and over. Queen Elizabeth weeps for her princes in the Tower in the most famous example, but the play is full of others. Elizabeth's older sons, from her first marriage, die at Richard's hands. Margaret is wracked with grief for her son Edward, dead in the battle at Tewkesbury. The Duchess of York mourns for her son Edmund, Earl of Rutland, killed before the play's action begins; for her son King Edward IV, who dies of an illness early in the play's action; for her son George, Duke of Clarence, murdered by Richard's hired hitmen; and for Richard himself, so awful she disowns him in a completely fantastic moment.

Aili's production invested in the power of the mothers' grief. Her production didn't have a heavy "concept," positioning the story in the 15th century. The one radical choice was in the cut; instead of silencing the women, she turned down everyone else. Many audience members familiar with the play said they had never seen a *Richard III* like this. Their response was visceral; every night patrons groaned and murmured and cheered as they watched the story unfold. The women's grief stoked their fire, which gave them power to move toward righting the world. The cut shifted the power in the story, but didn't fight the source material.

Richard III offers countless opportunities for reinterpretation—as do most good plays. Before you begin your cut, make sure you are extremely clear on your concept, your venue, your cast. Cut to enhance the production rather than trying to make the production fit your cut.

Tina Packer:
I think one of the things that has often happened in productions of *Richard III* is the women start getting slashed because they don't seem as important to the action and we can't bear those long lamentations. But lamentation was really important, and I think it's important for the audience to go through the lamentations as well. I know we're uncomfortable with all that grieving and wailing, but if the actors can really do it, it's amazing. Also if you start cutting all that stuff, you don't get the women as the opposition to Richard. The women actually unite with each other. So there's a whole layer of the play that if you start cutting it because you don't like it, because it's uncomfortable, I can't bear those bloody women, you're actually missing one section of the play. Maybe it just matters to me because I'm a woman, and therefore I don't want the women to be short changed. Maybe if you're doing *Richard* as kind of *derring-do* play, it doesn't really matter.

I started working out all the stuff about lamentation when I was a Bunting Fellow at Radcliffe. A couple of my Bunting sisters were working on lamentation (mostly from Greece, but then going over into the Renaissance) and the functions of lamentation and how the soul actually had to be carried from this world to the next. Unless the sound of the voice carried the soul, those souls couldn't get released into the next world. So I wouldn't cut any of it. Eventually, I cut little bits here and there, but I really took it as a demand on me to go quite far and strengthen the women. They are always the outsiders, so they're not only using lamentation as their way of creating their own power base, but as outsiders, they are commenting on the action of the male power structure.

7.9 Excerpt from interview with Tina Packer, 10 March 2021.

Works cited

Fain Lawrence-Edsell, Julie. *One Hour Shakespeare* (series). London: Routledge, 2020.
Jadhwani, Lavina. *Dismantling Anti-Black Linguistic Racism in Shakespeare: A Field Guide*. https://docs.google.com/document/d/1Kpq3nTAUVKwTrY_XLiH6aCr3ag UMu-pSCe87fg8DYQM/edit&sa=D&source=editors&ust=1614209217688000& usg=AOvVaw1wlkFzlBGfdzgDY5_ueQy0
Kaiser, Scott. *Have Shakespeare, Will Travel: Shakespearean Adaptations from the Oregon Shakespeare Festival's School Visit Program*. Oregon: Muse of Fire P, 2019.
Lopez, Jeremy. *Theatrical Convention and Audience Response in Early Modern Drama*. Cambridge: Cambridge UP, 2002.

Malone, Toby, and Aili Huber. "Cutting and Adapting Text for the Virtual Performing Landscape." *New & Noteworthy: The LMDA Newsletter* 6:4 (December 2020). N.p.

McKellen, Ian, and Richard Loncraine. *Richard III: The Screenplay*. London: Doubleday, 1996.

Packer, Tina. *Women of Will: The Remarkable Evolution of Shakespeare's Female Characters*. London: Penguin Random House, 2015.

8 Scissors, Paste, and Negotiations

Communicating Cuts

How and when will you share your cut with your collaborators? Cuts are, in nearly all cases, a *pre-production* activity. We front-load cuts in this way to ensure consistency and clarity from the first day of rehearsal. Of course, there are always exceptions. We heard about one outrageous production of *Hamlet* where the director asked the cast to fully memorize the entirety of the script, as presented in the Norton *Complete Works of Shakespeare* (a completist text if there ever was one), and then cut it to 90 minutes *in the process* of rehearsal. This is an abusive waste of the actors' time, both before and through rehearsal, and we would strongly advise against this approach. Rather, have your cut in hand well before tablework begins.

Usually, the cut is the responsibility of a select circle of artists, which often includes (but is not limited to) the dramaturg and the director, along with assistants and other interested parties. Often, a larger team can lead to a diluted focus, but it is different for every context. For example, both Kate Mulvany and Lue Douthit noted they incorporate lead actors into their cut process both *before* they start and *while* they work. Others work in isolation and only ask for feedback after they have a cut ready to read through. In nearly all cases, however, our experts agreed the script should be solid by the first rehearsal.

"Solid," of course, can be interpreted liberally: Martine Kei Green-Rogers described her practice, which both acknowledges collaboration yet keeps the onus for edits on the literary team: she presents a script with the majority of cuts finalized, and thus excised from the script entirely. The one exception is, "If we have *questions* about a line, we'll leave it in, with a strike-through." This offers actors the chance to play with the line on its feet. The creative team can decide together whether it belongs in their production. Kate Mulvany continues her revision process through rehearsal and even into performance: "As an adapter, I'm always checking in with the cast, well into the season, to ask, 'Is there anything you feel like you don't need? We can take it out if it's getting too exhausting.'" This on-the-fly process is unusual, but if the company is open to it, it can be invigorating.

DOI: 10.4324/9781003160076-9

Tina Packer:
When I first began, I never would cut a Shakespeare play until I'd worked on it for a couple of weeks, and then I'd say, "Now we can cut." By that time, we knew what was important. That was when we were very poor, and so we had the luxury of time. As the company's become more and more successful and costs have increased exponentially, rehearsal periods have become shorter and shorter.

At the beginning of the rehearsal process, I'd say we have to bring this down in a certain time, so that means there are going to be cuts, but we'll decide on what those cuts are together. Which I do try to do, and then, if there's no consensus, then I'll bring out my fascist side. But I didn't want to. I want to work *with* the actors, all the time. Now, we're often rehearsing three or four scenes concurrently, but at the end of the day, the whole group sits around and does a check-in about the insights that they discovered about the play today. So I'm always in dialogue with the whole cast about what the play is about. Some people discover really important things about very small exchanges. I don't want to cut those. If the actors come in and say, "No, this is really important," and I didn't see it, I'm certainly not going to cut it.

8.1 Excerpt from interview with Tina Packer, 10 March 2021.

Sharing your cut

The biggest choice in how you communicate cuts is whether to make it easy for the actors to see the lines you've excised.

You may decide to show the absent lines (cut lines are still visible under a strikethrough line or a highlight), to offer actors the full context. You may delete cut lines permanently, to demonstrate the finality of your cut. You might even choose to present multiple scripts in various stages of completion (one with cuts omitted, another with cuts visible). It's up to you.

Balancing the need for a rehearsal-ready text with the benefits of the whole story is always a challenge. You and your company should experiment to find the ideal method for you. We will share a few options that have worked for us.

A successful production will create easy opportunities to access the whole story, including parts that your actors will not stage. This is not always a given: on one occasion, in a talkback after a student production of *Much Ado About Nothing*, actors expressed confusion about why Claudio gets to marry Hero at the end. "He wasn't even really sorry," the actor who played Hero said. "I guess that's just how things were back then." While Claudio clearly

James Evans:
Opening it up to broad discussion is a big pitfall that I've decided we don't do anymore... I've learned that you come in with a pretty solid text and say, 'This is the text that we're using.'

One big mistake early on was leaving all the red bits turned on in "track changes" for the actor. Big mistake. That's the only bit they read!

8.2 Excerpt from interview with James Evans, 1 February 2021.

just barely deserves his redemption, the cut removed much of his apology to Leonato and the entire scene where he mourns Hero at her tomb. Removing both these scenes of remorse and redemption meant the storytelling was left with a gap: but what's more, the young cast had no idea what was cut. The actors were surprised to learn these details; they hadn't read the whole play. If the cast was familiar with the entire play prior to the start of rehearsal, they would have understood its resolution.

While actors *can* easily look up the text themselves, most *won't*. An actor who will read the entire play without being asked is a true asset to your company. With that said, it can be a serious challenge, even for these dedicated actors, to read a cut version and to follow the changes alongside a full text. It is not realistic to expect an actor to bounce back and forth between two texts at once; even if they did, some cuts are often not obvious, particularly if you've spackled the seams with a few new words, conflated characters, or reordered scenes. Despite the fact that an incurious actor might have no idea what they are missing, many directors prefer to ask their cast to focus on what is in front of them rather than what has been cut

Regardless of your presentation, it is standard to offer a version of the script correct as of the first day of rehearsal. Nearly all scripts evolve in some way or another in rehearsal and performance, and the stage manager will carefully record these changes in their "bible," or prompt book.

You might leave cut lines on the page, obscured by a stern strikethrough, as a reminder of what has been lost. This strategy has benefits and disadvantages. Usefully, an actor may mine struck-through material to inform their character and answer pertinent questions, which they may incorporate in their performance. A struck-through text can also complicate life for the stage manager or director—not only because it is a bother for actors, but also because many habitually use page count as a proxy for scene length, when planning rehearsal blocks. If a scene appears to be ten pages long, but three-quarters are cut, the schedule will be a mess. The strike-throughs also can complicate prompt-book compilation: some stage managers prefer to work with cut lines removed from these already-detailed texts so they may focus on their cue annotations.

Megan McDonough:
I can pull out a whole scene and giant chunks of the character beforehand: the actor's never going to be sad about it. They may even notice it if they go look at the script somewhere else, but they're not going to be sad about it. But if you make them draw lines in their script, all of a sudden it's precious, then they can't live without it. I have no problem with actors negotiating for something back in because usually it means I've missed something that's important to their character's arc. When you're cutting, you're trying to be 20 different souls on a journey, and you do your best, but the actor's the one embodying that one character and if there's something that I missed that they need, then I'm happy to hear an argument for putting that back in. I'm not happy to hear "I need this whole speech back in because I want to have more lines than the other guy," but that's rarely what actors are asking for.

8.3 Excerpt from interview with Megan McDonough, 9 February 2021.

What do actors prefer? In our experience, struck-through lines *can* offer useful context and serve as a fine repository for potential restorations, but they can also be busy on the page and difficult to read at a glance. Actually spoken text can get lost on the cluttered page, and stitched-together half-lines of verse can be difficult to track. Actors need a clear page. Take, for example, the difference between two presentations of the same cut of a scene from Hannah Cowley's *The Belle's Stratagem* (1780). Which would you rather act from?

Cuts marked:
LADY FRANCES: Sir George is going with me this morning ~~to the mercer's,~~ to chuse a silk; and then——
MRS. RACK: Chuse a silk for you! ha! ha! ha! Sir George chuses your laces too, I hope; your gloves, and your pincushions!
LADY FRANCES: Madam!
MRS. RACK: I am glad to see you blush, my dear Lady Frances. ~~These are strange homespun ways!~~ If you do these things, pray keep 'em secret. Lord bless us! If the Town should know your husband chuses your gowns!
MISS OGLE: You are very young, my Lady, and have been brought up in solitude. The maxims you learnt among the Wood-Nymphs in Shropshire, won't pass current here, I assure you.
MRS. RACK: Why, my dear creature, you look quite frighten'd!—Come, you shall go with us to an Exhibition, and an Auction.—Afterwards, we'll take a turn in the Park, and then drive to Kensington;—~~so we shall be at~~

122   *Scissors, Paste, and Negotiations*

~~home by four, to dress~~; and in the evening I'll attend you to Lady Brilliant's masquerade.
LADY FRANCES: I shall be very happy to be of your party, if Sir George has no engagements.
~~MRS. RACK: What! Do you stand so low in your own opinion, that you dare not trust yourself without Sir George! If you chuse to play Darby and Joan, my dear, you should have stay'd in the country;—'tis an Exhibition not calculated for London, I assure you!~~
MISS OGLE: What I suppose, my Lady, you and Sir George, will be seen pacing it comfortably round the Canal, arm and arm, ~~and then go lovingly into the same carriage;~~—dine tête-à-tête, ~~spend the evening at Picquet,~~ and so go soberly to bed at Eleven!—Such a snug plan may do for an Attorney and his Wife; but, for Lady Frances Touchwood, 'tis as unsuitable as linsey-woolsey,~~ or a black bonnet at the Festino~~!
LADY FRANCES: These are rather new doctrines to me!—But, my dear Mrs. Racket, you and Miss Ogle must judge of these things better than I can. As you observe, I am but young, and may have caught absurd opinions.—Here is Sir George!

Cuts excised:
LADY FRANCES: Sir George is going with me to chuse a silk; and then—
MRS. RACK: Chuse a silk for you! ha! ha! ha! Sir George chuses your laces too, I hope; your gloves, and your pincushions!
LADY FRANCES: Madam!
MRS. RACK: I am glad to see you blush, my dear Lady Frances. If you do these things, pray keep 'em secret. Lord bless us! If the Town should know your husband chuses your gowns!
MISS OGLE: You are very young, my Lady, and have been brought up in solitude. The maxims you learnt among the Wood-Nymphs in Shropshire, won't pass current here, I assure you.
MRS. RACK: Why, my dear creature, you look quite frighten'd! Come, you shall go with us to an Exhibition, and an Auction. Afterwards, we'll take a turn in the Park, and then drive to Kensington; and in the evening I'll attend you to Lady Brilliant's masquerade.
LADY FRANCES: I shall be very happy to be of your party, if Sir George has no engagements.
MISS OGLE: What I suppose, my Lady, you and Sir George, will be seen pacing it comfortably round the Canal, arm and arm, dine tête-à-tête, and so go soberly to bed at Eleven! Such a snug plan may do for an Attorney and his Wife; but, for Lady Frances Touchwood, 'tis as unsuitable as linsey-woolsey!
LADY FRANCES: These are rather new doctrines to me! But, my dear Mrs. Racket, you and Miss Ogle must judge of these things better than I can. As you observe, I am but young, and may have caught absurd opinions. Here is Sir George!

If you give actors rehearsal scripts with the cuts fully removed, offer them easy access to a script with the cuts marked. To some extent, how you create your cut will dictate how you share it.

- If you have marked out lines in a published book, you may scan or copy pages, so the actors get the full script and can see your pencil marks all over it.
- If you have transferred your script to a new document, you may choose to spend time in how you format your layout: this will include where you place your stage directions (italicized? Right-justified? In all-caps?) and font size. We strongly recommend you maintain a struck-through copy, an uncut copy, and a copy with your cuts expunged.
- You might like to keep a marked-up copy of the full script in the green room for easy perusal. If you worked digitally, an electronic version with strikethroughs is simple enough to share.
- If you have even moderate computer coding skills, a website version of the script with a button to show and hide the cut text can be useful for actors. Aili coded some tools to make this easy, available at www.cuttingplays.com.
- Not so computer-savvy? As we've already discussed, Toby presents his cuts in a much simpler parallel-text Excel spreadsheet form, which tracks iterations of the text over time, to mark when lines are cut and restored.

If nothing else, be sure to point actors to the copy text you used. For ancient and early modern texts, actors and production crew should always use the same text. An actor who uses the Arden when the cut is based on the Oxford is not necessarily using the same material.

As a sidebar: some artists shy away from published edition copy texts, as they can be messy and difficult to interpret. In the days prior to easy reproduction of text, the simplest way to distribute a cut was to supply a published edition, and to add cuts manually, often at a table read. Many impressively annotated prompt-books of the 18th and 19th century prompters and proto-stage managers are written over the top of published editions.

8.4 Software tools to facilitate cutting.

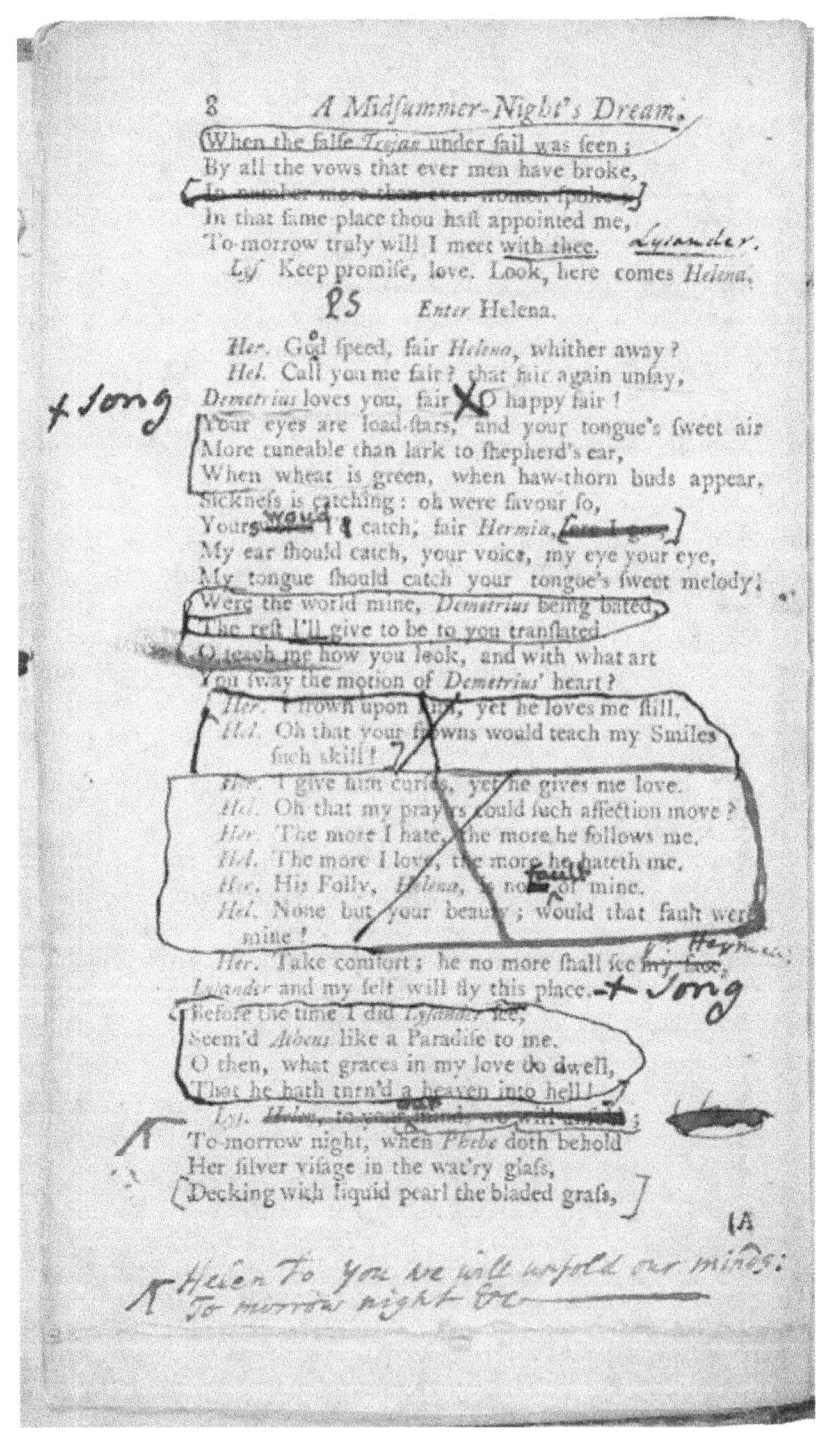

8.5 David Garrick's prompt book from his 1734 *A Midsummer Night's Dream* shows plenty of editorial intervention.

This meant all actors worked in the same text, and cuts were a simple pencil stroke (the more complex incorporated glue and scissors). Cuts were often based on performance editions from other artists, especially common through the Restoration period and into the 18th century, which meant many prompt books represented *cuts on top of cuts*. These artifacts, preserved both in physical and digital archives, offer glimpses into editorial choices and wonderful insight into such innovation.

Discussing cuts with cast

One fear you might have as you share the script with actors is that they may argue for lines "back." The power to grant these requests may be outside of your purview. Line restoration discussions typically happen between the director and the actor; if you are the dramaturg, you may be invited to weigh in, but the director usually makes the final call. Some directors have ironclad rules that actors may not request a line be reinstated. Others have a line barter system—an actor may have a line back, but only if they give up another one.

James Shapiro:
There's always a pushback on cuts. I did a cut for *Coriolanus* at the Royal Shakespeare Company four or five years ago. The experienced actors in the room would come in with their Ardens and say, "You cut my five best lines!" So I'd set up a table and do 'cap and trade'—if an actor wanted five lines they had to persuade another actor to give up five lines elsewhere. And because it was already three hours, they weren't going to go over [time], but because they wanted to restore those lines, they were making good arguments to restore them, just cut something else. So sometimes you have to manage those cuts in that creative way.

8.6 Excerpt from interview with James Shapiro, 8 February 2021.

Both stances reflect a rigidity out of step with the collaborative nature of the theatre. They may also cause problems with the cut itself. It should be a given that from time to time, you will make mistakes in your cut. You will cut lines which should not be cut. Or leave in others that don't make sense, vestigial organs you missed on your last pass through the text. An actor may notice this, where you did not, because it is their job to place their entire focus on the journey of a specific character. They will notice if, in your *The Marriage of Figaro* (1778), you cut the heart out of Figaro's climactic "inherited nobility" speech to save a little time. You should be gracious enough to listen to actors, and to thank them for their help in making the production better. They make *you* look good when they fix the gaps and gaffes in your version of the text.

"Line bartering" came up again and again in our interviews. This is even more open to danger than flat refusal. In a system where an actor can prioritize

8.7 James Evans of Bell Shakespeare (Australia) discusses his cut of *A Midsummer Night's Dream* with his Oberon, Kyle Morrison, for the 2021 national tour.

the importance of one line over another, a carefully constructed cut can come apart one line at a time. The actor's focus, again, is their specific character. They may not realize the line they want to give up sets up an important point of the broader story, or that it might facilitate another character's journey. The line they want back is less likely to cause trouble than the line they offer to give away, but remember: you cut it for a reason. This is not always obvious to the actor. We advise that you avoid this policy, especially if your role in the room is not one where you would be involved in these negotiations.

The best policy is to let actors ask for lines back. Facilitate a conversation about the reason the line is cut, and their desire to have it included. In our experience, most performers are nervous about being "*that* actor." They want to be "easy to work with." If they ask for a line back, they take a risk. Honor their courage and ask them why this line is worth the fight.

In Aili's production of *Richard III*, Katherine Mayberry, as Queen Elizabeth, asked to reinstate her response to Richard's oaths in Act Four, Scene Three:

RICHARD: Now, by my George, my garter, and my crown—
ELIZABETH: Profaned, dishonor'd, and the third usurp'd.

Aili had taken it out because she felt that if she kept it, the script then had to include Elizabeth's next speech: six lines to elaborate on the three items. The audience wouldn't know what a "George" or a "garter" were, so it seemed a good place to cut. Mayberry argued she could communicate her meaning without that little speech. "Profaned, dishonor'd, and the third usurp'd" was the launchpad into a section wherein Richard repeatedly tries to swear an oath, only to be continually interrupted as Elizabeth turns his language back on him. With the line restored, the scene was electric—one of the highlights of the play. Aili responded to Mayberry's observation that the line was a rhetorical pivot point and mirrored it with a turn in the scene's blocking. Nobody asked Mayberry to forfeit another line. That would have been a petty exercise, entirely beside the point. She earned this line, as she understood and articulated what it did for the scene better than anybody else in the room.

Anne Bogart:
Before going into rehearsal for SITI Company's production of *A Midsummer's Night Dream*, I spent a great deal of time and effort making radical cuts to the play. Then, over a rather painful first week of rehearsal, the actors systematically talked me into getting rid of almost ALL of the cuts. They were passionate and unrelenting. And this is how I learned that Shakespeare is an actor's playwright. Shakespeare belongs to actors, not to directors. Yes, a painful but good lesson.

In an ensemble, the actors have much more ownership of the process than with a pick-up group of actors. I find that actors in an ensemble do not simply accept the cuts, rather they propose alternatives or, as in the case of *A Midsummer's Night Dream*, they reject the cuts. Ultimately, their involvement makes for a much better production. In a number of other productions, I had to go into battle for the cuts that I made. Except for the experience with *A Midsummer's Night Dream*, the battles were always worth the effort.

8.8 Excerpt from interview with Anne Bogart, 8 March 2021.

Obviously, you may encounter an actor who demands lines back for less valid reasons. In our experience, these folks are rare, but they do appear from time to time. We find the best strategy is simply to treat them as reasonable collaborators. Don't assume they're difficult or pushy. They may not understand the purpose of the text cut at all. If they ask why a line was cut, offer an explanation. Be gracious but firm, and be ready to learn you made a mistake.

Your actors, particularly if they are not accustomed to public domain texts, may not know cuts are common. They might not be aware of the instability of play texts. A preemptive discussion with your creative team is vital. Be sure everyone understands that play cuts are common practice and the concept of a sacrosanct text is a modern invention. Explain some of the choices you made in this cut to shape the story, solve a personnel problem, accommodate a space, or build out a director's concept. Note any places where characters are conflated, and discuss how this changes the characters' development. When they see the sacrificed lines as part of a bigger whole, as a way in which you care for them, for the audience, and for the production, they're more likely to buy into it. If they do request a line be reinstated, they will understand the larger context and may help *you* understand how it contributes to the vision you've laid out.

As in all things, communication is key. If actors feel like you've crept in and stolen words from them under the cover of darkness, they may feel the need to hoard lines and ask for more. If they see cuts as a collaborative act, they'll find a way to collaborate with you.

Discussing cuts with the audience or the public

Unless your cut radically diverges from the play your audience expects to see, the vast majority of your viewers will not notice where you've cut. Or even *if* you've cut. If you leave in the key famous lines, it's a good bet they will be entirely oblivious.

Some people, though, absolutely *will* notice. A surprising number of the experts we interviewed remembered people in the audience who followed along with their Penguin (or similar) editions. These audience members can be difficult to convince of the validity of text cuts. Peter Brook even mentions them in *The Empty Space*:

> There is always a deadly spectator, who, for special reasons enjoys a lack of intensity and even a lack of entertainment, such as the scholar who emerges from routine performances of the classics smiling because nothing has distracted him from trying over and confirming his pet theories to himself, whilst reciting his favorite lines under his breath. (10)

For these "deadly spectators," does it help to know what has been cut, or what a cut looks like?

Often, audiences aren't particularly aware of a cut. Nonetheless, when the topic is broached, it can be a source of some interest, if not faux outrage, at the audacity that a script would be subjected to such indignity. If you have spent time on your script cut, or have engaged an artist to do so, acknowledge this labor in the show program or playbill. This role could be credited in a number of different ways: text editor, text dramaturg, cut coordinator, text consultant. But what if it wasn't their main job? Surely they don't need credit then? If the director cuts the play, by the time they get to production, who cares? Or if your production dramaturg had a hand in the cut, there's no need for credit, since this falls under the job description of dramaturg, right? We disagree. When a company credits the cutter, they advertise the specificity of this job. Audience members will read their programs, and perhaps one or two, knowledgeable enough about the play to notice there have been some changes, will know whom to praise. Or blame…

This is more than a simple ego advertisement. Credit normalizes the importance of text cuts to most productions of public domain plays, and reminds companies and artists this is a role which cannot be underestimated. Cutting is more than a matter of a few slashes before you call it a day: it is responsive, active, detailed work just as important in pre-production as sourcing props or hemming costumes.

Program credit should be a given, but be warned: most well-intentioned companies forget. This isn't any reflection on your work. It's a reflection on habits built over years of repetition. Until the late 19th century, and even into the 20th century, the *director* was an afterthought too: it was not until it was normalized that it became standard. Speak to the producer to request acknowledgement for however you prefer to be credited, be it text editor, or text cutter, or dramaturg, or even add a slash, which might look like "Dramaturg/Text Editor" or "Assistant Director/Script Cutter," to draw attention to your hard work.

This credit may elicit queries, especially in the useful theatrical forum of the talkback. A post-show (sometimes pre-show) talkback is a facilitated conversation between artists and the audience. Often, a producer, dramaturg, or education manager offers insight into the production. Actors, designers, technicians, and other members of the production team participate in these talkbacks, which may stray into the area of your cut. In many cases, the conversation will proceed like this:

MODERATOR: Are there any questions?
AUDIENCE MEMBER: Yes! I have one. *How could you* cut all those lines?
MODERATOR: Which lines?
AUDIENCE MEMBER: The lines! In Nora's 'You have never loved me' speech!
ACTOR PLAYING NORA (*not really joking*): Tell me about it!
    (*laughter*)

Cuts are, by their nature, a process of reduction. Often, people react with incredulity at a cut in a beloved speech, and sometimes receive support from the actor who lost those lines. For this reason, you should continually communicate the purpose of your cuts to your company, so when such a question arises they will offer a better answer than, "Tell me about it," while you simmer balefully in the audience. If your Nora knows her lines were cut to highlight the pathos in the speech, she can communicate this. If you did not communicate the purpose of those cuts to the company—if you were the type of cutter who delivered new pages without explanation or apology—you are at the mercy of an actor who assumes you cut their lines because you're a nasty person.

It's vital your actors understand the purpose of your cuts and don't undermine them. We once heard a talkback after a *Romeo and Juliet* cut *conservatively* for a high school audience. An actor remarked that most of the dirty bits had been removed, and for a more adult version, the students, some of whom were pupils at a religious school, should return for a performance that night, which used a longer version of the script. Clearly, the text editor didn't do a good enough job to help the actor understand *why* they'd removed those lines for *this* audience.

Sometimes, wonderfully, you might even find yourself on the talkback stage yourself, perhaps as a dramaturg, moderator, or another production role, and you can speak to the process. No one can communicate the purpose of your cuts better than you can. You should also offer to participate in educational outreach, which might include interviews, publicity, or, most commonly, a program note. A program often features dramaturgical insight, and if your company has space for a dramaturg's note in addition to the director's note, take the chance to offer a sense of your approach to the text.

Ultimately, your text should speak for itself. The cut is the tool that shapes the raw material of the text into what the actors speak and enliven on stage. If you can effectively communicate the story through your cut, you may find no one notices at all. More likely, audience members will see the credit for a text editor, but will be unable to identify what is gone. Sometimes large, audacious cuts or rearrangements get the audience's attention, but most often it's microsurgery: a line here, a paragraph there, merge two servants but don't make a fuss. If your cut was strong enough to tell the story and your audience can't see the seams, you're on the right track. You always run the risk of an expert in the audience gasping horrified at your choices, but the people who attend the theatre to pick holes in the cut aren't there to have fun anyway.

If you follow your process throughout, select your copy text with care, justify moments, brave a test read, table work, and rehearsal, your cut is most likely robust enough to stand up to scrutiny. The intention behind any cut is to communicate your approach to the play *right now*. It's not necessarily meant to be eternal or timeless. It's never a matter of comparison ("Oh no, the company across town has the same play but ten minutes shorter!"). Your script fills the need you and your company had to entertain your audience. As far as we're concerned, the best way to cut a play is to get started. As Beckett said, "Ever tried. Ever failed. No matter. Fail again. Fail better." Theatre is a living beast which requires different approaches at different times, and cutting text is not easy. Try it. Cut it up and read it out. Find out what you need. Fail again.

Fail better.

Works cited

Beckett, Samuel. *Worstward Ho!* London: Grove P, 1983.
Brook, Peter. *The Empty Space.* New York: Atheneum, 1968.
Malone, Toby. "Digital Parallel-Text Approaches to Performance Historiography." *Shakespeare's Language in Digital Media: Old Words, New Tools*, edited by Janelle Jenstad, Jennifer Roberts-Smith, Mark Kaethler. London: Routledge, 2017, pp. 105–123.

Appendix 1
Legal Concerns

Maybe you have a great idea for a one-hour *Waiting For Godot*. Or an Australian-set *Glengarry Glen Ross*. Or a two-hander *Angels in America*. You want to be fully informed about what you can and can't do with a script under copyright. Spoiler: in each of these cases, you'd receive a flat refusal from the rights holder, and if you went ahead anyway, you would run the risk of a cease-and-desist order, and/or escalating legal action. While we enthusiastically believe a cut can improve a performance text, we want to make it extremely clear *there are some scripts you cannot cut.* Each play we use as an example is in the public domain in the United States, Canada, and the United Kingdom. Intellectual property laws differ from one country to another, but all nations have laws to protect playwrights' creations. Be sure to research the public domain laws in your country.

What is copyright?

Copyright, in extremely simple terms, is *the right to copy*. A person or group of people who create a new piece of art own that creation and only they, or those they authorize, are legally permitted to copy, profit from, or change it. Most countries protect copyright for a certain period of time to incentivize creation of new work. If a playwright's work could be produced immediately upon publication, without payment, the playwright might find it difficult to generate any sort of income. The government protects the playwright's ownership of their ideas, so they can earn money, which, if the playwrights we know are any measure, they will immediately spend on tea and development for their next play. However, copyrights are not protected indefinitely. Laws vary from one country to another, but, in general, works enter the public domain around 70 years after the death of the creator.

What is the public domain?

The *public domain* comprises creations not protected by copyrights, patents, or trademarks. Anyone can use or modify public domain work, without permission, but no one can claim to own it. However, *modifications* to a public domain work may be protected by copyright. This means *your cut* of a public domain play can be copyrighted, and if you copyright it, others must request your permission to perform it. You may choose to request a royalty for this type of use.

Violations of copyright

Shows get shut down every year due to copyright violations. When you sign a license agreement with a rights holder, you agree to perform the play *exactly as written*. What this means can vary from one rights holder to another, but this will be specified in the contract. While some playwrights are flexible about cast, many expect your cast to match the characters as written (no re-gendered characters, for example). In some cases, productions have been shut down for even the mildest expression of artistic license. A famous example is a 2017 Oregon production of *Who's Afraid of Virginia Woolf* denied performance rights because director Michael Streeter wanted to cast a Black actor as Nick. The Albee estate rejected this choice because, in the words of Albee's former agent, Jonathan Lomma,

> While it has been established that non-Caucasian actors in different combinations have played all the roles in the play at various times with Edward's approval, he was consistently wary of directors attempting to use his work to provide their own commentary by, for instance, casting only Nick as non-white, which essentially transforms George and Martha into older white racists, which is not what Edward's play is about.

In other cases, when the playwright has not been explicit about production choices, they've been frustrated with surprise developments, like one university production of *To the Mountaintop* which cast a white man as Dr. Martin Luther King, Jr. For the record, playwright Katori Hall has spoken publicly about her disapproval of this choice and subsequently added a clause to the play's licensing agreement to specify the character's race.

Productions run afoul of their licensing agreements in minor, but still legally actionable ways. It is absolutely illegal to cut copyrighted play texts *at all* without permission.

You can't cut a song that is too difficult for your actor. You can't get rid of a character who doesn't add much to the story and whom you have trouble casting. You can't take out a scene which revolves around a special effect you aren't able to create. Educational environments commonly cut references to drugs and alcohol, or switch "damn" to "darn," yet this is *still illegal*. If you can't say the "old familiar suggestion" onstage at your school, you'd better not try to do Mamet. Your audience may not understand the 1950s references in *Guys and Dolls*, but this doesn't mean you can update them to contemporary products and terms (this sounds like a joke: we've seen it done).

You also cannot *add* anything. If your clown ad libs a funny line in rehearsal, you cannot keep it in performance. If you feel like a point of the

Caridad Svich:
I wasn't in the same city as this production was happening, but I said, "I'll come in a few weeks in and see how it's going." When I got to town, they told me, "We're going to watch a run." I was watching it and I had no idea what was going on. I literally didn't know where we were. It was completely out of order. Some things were cut. Some things were looped. It was completely rearranged. I had to leave the room.

On another show, also in a city far from where I live, around tech, I got a rehearsal report that said, "We crossed out a bunch of scenes." The initial excuse was that they were touring the show to schools, and it was too long, so they had to cut it. I wish I had known that before, I would have done a cut of the play. But later, I contacted the director, and he told me, "Oh, no we actually cut things for other reasons. You wrote a song in, and the actor couldn't sing." The music of the show is super important; it's the one thing I'm responsible for. It's the architecture of the piece. When you're moving pieces of the architecture around, it feels like a violation. I'm all for trying things in the room, but don't send me stuff with stuff crossed out. I knew that the scenes that were cut were the pivotal plot point. I kept thinking of audiences seeing the show and not understanding how we got from one point to another. I don't want audiences seeing this and thinking it was what was agreed upon by all parties involved.

A1.1 Excerpt from interview with Caridad Svich, 5 February 2021.

action is unclear and you want to add a narrator and frame for it… you can't. We once saw a misguided student production of *The Intruder* which cast an extra actor to play the unseen spirit of death that stalks the play. Death sneaked around the stage and clarified his identity in a new epilogue speech just in case the audience missed it. It entirely changed (ruined?) the play, but Maurice Maeterlinck has been dead since 1949, so there was no recourse for action aside from audience grumbles. That play is in the public domain; creators can do whatever they want with it. For plays still under licensing agreements, the performance text must be exactly as the playwright created it.

It is for this reason that advocacy groups, unions, and trade associations exist: to defend the playwright's rights and their work. The Dramatists' Guild of America, who bill themselves as "the nation's first and only trade association for American theatre writers," can point to a codified Bill of Rights (https://www.dramatistsguild.com/rights), which includes the provision that they can expect "artistic integrity" around how playwrights' work is addressed. This means "No one (e.g., producers, directors, actors, designers,

134 *Legal Concerns*

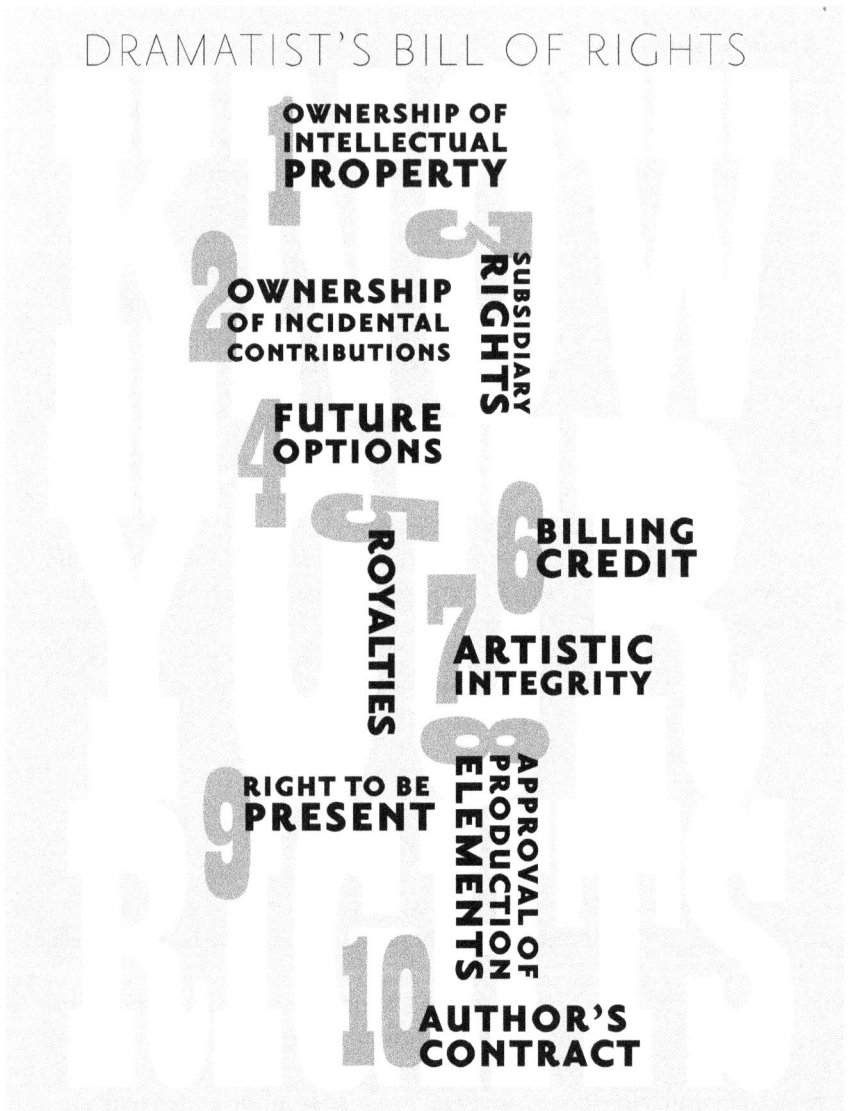

A1.2 The Dramatists Guild of America Bill of Rights. Artwork Design by Bekka Lindstrom used with permission from The Dramatists Guild of America, the national trade association playwrights, composers, lyricists, and librettists.

dramaturgs) can make additions, deletions, alterations, and/or changes of any kind to your script – including the text, title, and stage directions – without your prior written consent." That means if you're handling a play that is not in the public domain, and you do not have this written consent, then you cannot make changes.

Since we are hopeless pedants and valiant defenders of intellectual property, we *also* want to note that you cannot copy costume designs, choreography, directorial concept, or any number of other pieces of intellectual property from another production (or film) without permission. Some play licenses include permission to use floor plans from the original production. Others specify a requirement to use (and pay for) the official poster image for the show. If the licensing agreement does not specifically include permission to use something from the original production, you must not use it. You can't copy the dance numbers from the *West Side Story* movie unless you pay Jerome Robbins' estate. If you duplicate Cinderella's dress, you might hear from the House of Mouse. Theatrical productions are multilayered artistic creations; you can only use what you have licensed.

Translations

One pitfall we have seen companies stumble into is that copyright applies to *translations* of plays. Just as you could copyright your cut of a play, so the translator can copyright their translation. *The Grouch*, Ranjit Bolt's 2008 translation of *The Misanthrope* (1666), for example, is *not* a public domain play, despite the original work being more than 350 years old. Public domain translations of many classical plays exist; check the date *of the translation*, not the play's original composition.

Whom does this hurt?

One argument for cuts to licensed plays is that it doesn't harm anybody and might even be beneficial. *If my students at our all-male institution will only get to experience* Far Away *if I change the genders of a few characters, isn't it worth putting a toe across the line in the legal sand? It's not like this hurts Caryl Churchill at all...*

The problem is, it does. A playwright lives with their creation for years before it ever sees the stage. They've thought about the various possibilities for bringing it to life. They haven't created the characters at random. If you make a change, you might damage the interwoven structure of the play in ways you can't see at the outset. Playwrights live by their reputation. If a lukewarm review results from your changes, which the reviewer assumes are original to the script, this might lead to other theatres not producing the play.

We also want to note: a playwright's reputation deserves protection even after their plays enter the public domain. Although you are legally free to do whatever you want to a 300-year-old play, a program note on these changes is helpful to others who may be curious. Your freewheeling adaptation isn't going to hurt Shakespeare, but might prevent other theatres from taking up Sor Juana Inés de la Cruz.

How does it hurt you when your play is changed?
TJ Young:
A producer that I was working with before I knew my rights [to have the final say on cuts]...I wrote this show that was two acts, and they knew it was two acts, because it was the first piece of theater that I wrote that they saw. They had seen it before! They had me cut it down to 90 minutes, and because they made me do it in a hurry, I removed two scenes. In the review, they said, "I feel like X, Y, and Z were missing." Those things that were missing were in those two scenes they made me cut. Now I have a lukewarm review for something that would have worked otherwise.

A1.3 Excerpt from interview with TJ Young, 9 February 2021.

How will anyone ever find out?

We have heard producers argue nobody will ever find out about the innocent excision they made to remove the racist comments from a production of *You Can't Take It With You* (1936) in a community theatre in a small town far from the geographic centers of the theatre world. The cuts make the play more palatable for their performers and audience. How would they ever get caught?

Adherence to the law should never be predicated on what you think you can get away with, and in the present era, you can't get away with much. Rights agencies, like Dramatists Play Service, Samuel French, or Musical Theatre International handle licensing for most plays. They have rooms full of lawyers whose entire job is to find productions which violate their copyright and send strongly worded letters, sometimes followed by litigation. If you plan to advertise your show at all, whether on social media or in your local paper, those lawyers will get an automated notification. Anything particularly out of the ordinary will draw their attention. *Hair* at an elementary school? They'll want to know if you plan to cut every song but "Let the Sun Shine In." If so, have you contacted them for permission? An *Avenue Q* at a conservative Christian university? Expect some scrutiny. The presently unavailable *Hadestown* based on a bootleg video you found on YouTube? Resist the temptation.

Even if the pairing of your institution with the script doesn't raise any obvious red flags, don't expect to make minor edits no one notices. Sure, you may have previously worked on an unauthorized adaptation on the downlow before, and no one noticed. Rights holders have the authority to check in on every production they license, which is why in the contract you sign there are often provisions where the licenser is entitled to tickets, should they choose to come. They usually don't use them, because they license hundreds of productions every week. The problem is the one day the licenser randomly selects your production for review, or when the playwright, who receives a notification of every production of their play, realizes their favorite aunt lives in your town and decides to make the trip to check it out. It is much, much harder to restore a script to its licensed version than it is to adhere to the rules at the outset of the process. We saw one production illegally cross-gender cast a Martin McDonough play, explicitly in contravention of the license agreement. No one noticed until the play was submitted for Festival consideration. The Festival respondent noted the irregularity and the institution was forced to withdraw their application lest the higher-profile appearance at the regional Festival drew the rights holders' attention. If you break the rules 100 times and get away with it 99 of those times, that one legal strike is enough to bring down a theatre company or drama department. *Don't risk it.*

It might also go without saying, but our reference to contracts and licensing is not incidental. If you have decided you want to stage *Hamilton* with your friends and think it's so unfair the rights aren't available yet, your underground friends-only staging has broken the law. You've found a script online and want to perform the play with the Broadway cast recording you bought from iTunes? If word leaks out to the rights holders (Lin-Manuel Miranda is rightly *very* protective of how his intellectual property is distributed), you will be shut down, at great legal cost to you. All of this is to say that when you sign the rights contract for your performance—and you MUST sign a rights contract for plays not in the public domain—please, do yourself a favor and read every word. The last thing you want is to be shut down on the off-chance a licensing rep decides to ensure your play is consistent.

There are examples of litigation which waded into a gray area of content, such as the 2003 50th anniversary production of *Waiting for Godot* in Sydney. In this high-profile case, the Beckett estate was outraged over the addition of percussive Latin drums to the production. Edward Beckett, the playwright's nephew, claimed the production was in violation of its contract in the use of "unauthorized music," an accusation vehemently denied by director Neil Armfield, who in a moment of pique branded Edward Beckett "an enemy of art" and insisted no such provision existed in the contract they signed (Molloy 93–94). Regardless of who was an enemy of whom, clearly, changes must be made mindfully.

In 2019, Samuel French published a short play written by David Lindsay-Abaire entitled *Can I Change the Words or Music?*, designed as a dialogue guide for theatre educators. The very fact that Samuel French saw a need for such a product clearly shows that enough license holders change text and lyrics, unaware of the legality of the decision.

Spoiler for this short play: No, you can't.

Versions

While we are on the subject of contracts, be sure you perform the script you are licensed to perform. Edward Albee, in his twilight years, wrote *Homelife* (2004), a prequel to his 1959 one-act play *The Zoo Story*. Subsequently,

Albee announced *The Zoo Story* was no longer available to be performed as a standalone play, but should be combined with *Homelife* to create a full-length play, usually staged as *At Home at the Zoo*. Albee responded to protests over the inability to stage the classic *Zoo Story* alone by saying it was *his* play, and he could do what he wanted with it. He's right. Neil LaBute specifically revised *The Shape of Things* after the development of the 2003 film version, which removed certain scenes and entirely changed the play's final moment. Always stage the version you are licensed for, regardless of what it says in the paperback you picked up second hand.

Many plays have official cuts which you can license. Musical theatre International offers a series of "Junior" versions of various musicals (such as *Seussical Jr., Oklahoma Jr.,* and *Grease Jr.*). These official cuts generally transpose difficult songs into more singable keys, cut controversial or complicated material, and shorten the overall runtime, in order to make them more accessible for middle and high school performers. Another common official cut is the competition cut, which takes a full-length play and slices it down to a 40-minute runtime for competitions like the International Thespians. These cuts are often prepared by the playwright, and therefore have their approval.

Exceptions

One major exception: you can make changes *with permission*. If you receive written permission from the rights holder, you're on the right side of the law. Your licensing agreement should include contact information for exactly these sorts of appeals. Playwrights are often happy to work with you on changes which would make or break a production for your particular context. Some playwrights' estates are notoriously difficult to work with, but for the most part, they are flexible. It's worth the ask.

Let's return, for a moment, to the Albee estate's denial of rights for a production of *Who's Afraid of Virginia Woolf?* with a Black actor. In fact, Albee himself approved such a production at Howard University in 2001. Director Vera Katz wrote to Albee to request two minor script changes in order to make the play work for an all-Black cast. Albee called her and suggested further changes, 13 in all. He traveled to Howard, met the student actors, and discussed the play with them. What could have been a disaster in the courts of law (for Howard University theatre) and of public opinion (for Albee) turned out to be a success for all involved—because Katz had the temerity to request permission and collaboration from a giant of the American theatre.

We want to encourage your creativity and offer you tools for modifying playscripts to carry out your artistic vision. But under no circumstances do we condone violation of another artist's intellectual property rights.

What about my cut? Is it mine?

If you have completed a successful cut of a play, you may wonder whether it now belongs to you. Playwright Peter Oswald confided a story about how, in his translation of *Don Carlos* (1787), his performance cuts were based on a prior cut by another director. When, by chance, this director discovered his cuts had been adopted, he promised a call from his agent, to protect his intellectual property. This is a thorny subject: no text cutter is likely to claim they "own" an individual textual cut, such as the rearrangement of scenes or omission of lines. There is no real way to be sure they were the first to think of conflating two characters or trimming an 18-line speech to six. In the larger scale, however, if a cut is materially and structurally the same—if a cutter has found an edition on the internet and has decided to take it for themselves but hasn't acknowledged the originator—then this is more of an issue. As it stood, Oswald's *Don Carlos* used the other version as a guide, but did not follow it step by step. Part of the process of theatre is putting things out into the world, so it is inevitable that if something succeeds, others may mimic it. If you were to adopt, without acknowledgement, the entire content of *The Marowitz Macbeth*—a cut-and-paste adaptation of which the Daily Telegraph's Eric Shorter famously said, "Shakespeare may be able to take it. But can we?" (qtd in Ellis)—which is such a radical cut it's essentially a new play, you'd be in trouble. To take this cut and present it as something new is problematic. There is no explicit protection for this, since it's editorial intervention on a pre-existent script, but be aware of this grey area when you share a cut.

Works cited

Ellis, Samantha. "Macbeth, London, 1969." *The Guardian*. 19 November 2003. https://www.theguardian.com/stage/2003/nov/19/theatre

Katz, Vera J. "Who's Afraid of Virginia Woolf and Race?" *Eclectique1916*. http://www.eclectique916.com/2017/06/05/whos-afraid-of-virginia-woolf-and-race/

Lindsay-Abaire, David. *Can I Change the Words or Music?* New York: Samuel French, 2019.

Molloy, Frank. "The Director versus the Playwright: Samuel Beckett Goes 'Down Under'". *Hungarian Journal of English and American Studies (HJEAS)* 10:½ (Spring/Fall, 2004), pp. 89–97. https://www.jstor.org/stable/41274266

Appendix 2
Cut Activities

As a practical exercise, select a play you're interested in working on. Together, we are going to envision a possible cut version of that play, including selecting some scenes for hands-on slicing and dicing.

If you don't have a play in mind, select a potential scene from the provided list at http://www.cuttingplays.com/scenes.

History

Playtext in hand, examine the actual document you're working with.

- Where did it come from, and how did it get to you?
- Who edited it? In what year were they doing their scholarship?
- Can you find out what version of the play text the editor was working from? What other options did they have to choose from? What are key differences between these scripts?

The Three Questions

If you have an impending performance, consider it as you revisit the Three Questions. Alternatively, visit http://www.cuttingplays.com/randomizer to generate a random performance scenario.

Once you have answered these three questions, reflect on your play as a whole. Do the answers here point to any obvious cuts? Are there entire scenes that won't fit in this production?

- Who is your audience?
    - What are their demographics?
        - Age range
        - Education
        - Socio-economic status

- Race and ethnicity
  - Rural, urban, suburban
- How much do they know about this play, playwright, style or era of theater, and genre?
- Why are they coming to your show?
- What is their relationship to theater, generally, and to *your* theater particularly?
- What do they expect to see? How will they feel if their expectations are not met?
- What is your story?
  - What is each core character's story?
  - What is the story of each scene?
- How much time do you have?
  - How much play text does that allow you?
  - How much of this play do you need to eliminate?

Materials

Now it's time to decide how you will create your cut. Find a good pencil, or set up a computer file to receive your cut. Decide on what format your copy text will be in: are you copying a text from the internet and pasting it into a document? Cutting in a paperback? Prepare before you start to cut, or you may live to regret it.

- How will you make your cuts clear, but reversible?
- How will you calculate your time/line count?

Strategies

From here on, limit your scope to just one scene of your play. Pick one that you wouldn't eliminate entirely, but which will require some trimming in order to fit your production.

- What does your scene need? What are the crucial plot elements the scene provides to the play overall?
- Are you doubling any roles in your production? Do you need to adjust your cut to prevent an actor traffic jam?
- Are there any words you should replace because they are offensive or obscure?
- Would this scene benefit from rearrangement or merging with another scene?
- Are there big chunks you should take out? Are there lines that need minor adjustment?

Character

Think about this scene with a particular eye to each character's overall journey, as well as their contribution to this scene.

- Can any characters be conflated?
- Is one character dominating the scene? Can you support or undercut that pattern?
- Are any of the characters in the scene extraneous? How will the scene change if you remove them?

Mechanics

It's time to get to the nitty-gritty nuts and bolts of the scene. The playwright carefully selected each word in this scene; make sure you know why before you cut them.

- Is your text in verse or prose? A combination? Why?
- What do characters' patterns of language tell you about them?
- What are the rhetorical hallmarks of your playwright?

Production

To get a real feel for how production alters a cut, visit our random production generator and come up with another production concept for contrast. Don't worry if it's far from something that you might consider for your production. Cut your scene twice—how are these cuts different from each other? What does this show you about what is core to your story?

Communicating

Now that you've got your scene cut, share it with somebody. Are you going to show them your cut with struck out lines? A carefully redacted, nicely formatted print out? Something in between?

Invite a group of friends to read the cut aloud and discuss it. How does it hit your ear? Are there jumps in the logic that your actors question? Consider what changes you'll make in your next draft.

Appendix 3
Further Reading

Block, Giles. *Speaking the Speech: An Actor's Guide to Shakespeare*. London: Nick Hern, 2013.
Crystal, David, and Ben Crystal. *Shakespeare's Words: A Glossary and Language Companion*. London: Penguin, 2002.
Fain Lawrence-Edsell, Julie. *One Hour Shakespeare* (series). London: Routledge, 2020.
Gooch, Steve. *The Cut Shakespeare*. https://www.stevegooch.info/thecut/
Hartley, Andrew James. *The Shakespearean Dramaturg: A Theoretical and Practical Guide*. London: Palgrave, 2005.
Hinman, Charlton, ed. *The First Folio of Shakespeare*. New York: Paul Hamlyn, 1968.
Hutcheon, Linda. *A Theory of Adaptation: Second Edition*. New York: Routledge, 2013.
Kaiser, Scott. *Have Shakespeare, Will Travel: Shakespearean Adaptations from the Oregon Shakespeare Festival's School Visit Program*. Oregon: Muse of Fire P, 2019.
Kermode, Frank. *Shakespeare's Language*. London: Penguin, 2001.
Lindsay-Abaire, David. *Can I Change the Words or Music?* New York: Samuel French, 2019.
Marowitz, Charles. *The Marowitz Shakespeare: Adaptions* (sic) *and Collages of Hamlet, MacBeth, the Taming of the Shrew, Measure for Measure, and the Merchant of Venice*. London: Drama Publishers, 1979.
Rasmussen, Eric. *A Textual Companion to 'Dr Faustus'*. Manchester: Manchester UP, 1993.
Smith, Bruce R. *Shakespeare / Cut: Rethinking Cutwork in an Age of Distraction*. Oxford: Oxford UP, 2016.
Taylor, Gary. *Reinventing Shakespeare: A Cultural History from the Restoration to the Present*. Oxford and New York: Oxford UP, 1991.
Taylor, Gary, and Michael Warren, eds. *The Division of the Kingdoms: Shakespeare's Two Versions of King Lear*. Oxford: Oxford UP, 1987.
Wright, George. *Shakespeare's Metrical Art*. Berkeley: U California P, 1991.

Digital resources

Cutting Plays: The Official Companion Site to *Cutting Plays for Performance: A Practical and Accessible Guide*. www.cuttingplays.com

Digital Renaissance Editions: Digital Texts of Early English Drama, Including Many Obscurities. https://digitalrenaissance.uvic.ca/

The Dramatists Guild of America Bill of Rights. https://www.dramatistsguild.com/rights

Folger Shakespeare: Open-source Editions of Shakespeare's Works. https://shakespeare.folger.edu/

Internet Shakespeare Editions: Peer-reviewed Multi-text Editions of Shakespeare's Works. https://internetshakespeare.uvic.ca/

MIT Shakespeare: Unannotated Editions of Shakespeare's Works. http://shakespeare.mit.edu/

Project Gutenberg: Extensive Online Resources for Works in the Public Domain. https://www.gutenberg.org/

Queen's Men Editions: Peer-reviewed Editions of Play by Shakespeare's Contemporaries, Specifically Those Performed by the Queen's Men Troupe. https://qme.uvic.ca/

Shakespeare's Words: Interactive Shakespearean Lexicon and Dictionary. www.shakespeareswords.com

Theoi Classical Texts Library: Greek and Roman Texts. https://www.theoi.com/Library.html

Wilde Online: The Works of Oscar Wilde. https://www.wilde-online.info/plays.html

Index

actors' parts 10–11, 64
adaptation 13, 20, 52, 56, 101, 111
Aeschylus 1, 57
Albee, Edward 132, 137–138
Aldridge, Ira xiii, 7, 26
American Shakespeare Center (Staunton, VA), The xiii, 32, 86, 103, 113
Ancient Greece 10, 108, 116
annotations 36, 43, 45, 46, 120
Antonio's Revenge (Marston) 94
Antony and Cleopatra (Shakespeare) xiii, 34
As You Like It (Shakespeare) 17–18, 22
At Home at the Zoo (Albee) 138

Bartholomew Fair (Jonson) 18
Barton, John 55–56, 60
Beckett, Samuel 130, 131, 137
Bell Shakespeare (Australia) 107, 111, 126
Belle's Stratagem, The (Cowley) 121
Bells, The (Lewis) 5
Black Doctor, The (Aldridge) 7, 26
Blackfriars Playhouse, Virginia xiii, 103
Bogart, Anne 8, 127
Bold Stroke for a Husband, A (Cowley) 45
Bold Stroke for a Wife, A (Centlivre) 7, 90–92, 93, 95-96
Booth, Stephen 92
Bowdler, Thomas 58
Bracknell, Kylie (Kaarljiilba Kaardn) 107–108
Branagh, Kenneth 19, 23

Carroll, Tim 6, 8, 19, 22, 55, 58, 89–90, 100
casting 56–57, 67–68, 72–74, 99–102, 137
Centlivre, Susanna xiii, 7, 90–92, 93, 95-96

character removal 66–71
Chekhov, Anton 24, 25, 55, 97, 101, 110
Cimolino, Antoni 5, 18, 19, 35, 42, 49, 50, 59, 95, 104
Cohen, Amy R. 15
Cohen, Ralph Alan 32, 66, 71, 76, 92
Comedy of Errors, The (Shakespeare) 10, 11
concept 1, 7, 23, 30, 38, 48, 59, 68, 97–99, 102–103, 109, 111–115, 127, 135, 142
conflation; character 8–9, 42, 71–74, 114, 120, 127–128, 139, 142
conflation; plays 64, 75
conflation; texts 45, 64, 75–76
Congreve, William 19, 52, 94, 95
context 2–5, 16, 36, 43, 46–47, 49, 67, 72, 74, 81, 84, 95, 96, 97–99, 100, 103, 105, 110–111, 119, 121, 128
copy text 38, 40–44, 46, 47, 123, 130, 141
copyright 7, 13, 131–135
Coriolanus (Shakespeare) xiii, 59, 125
COVID-19 68, 98, 108

Der Bestrafte Brudermord (Fratricide Punished) (Anonymous) 13
design 3, 8, 23, 52, 98, 99, 101, 104, 107–108, 111–112, 129, 133–134, 135
digital tools 36, 37, 46–47, 123, 125, 144
discussing cuts with audiences 128–130
Doll's House, A (Ibsen) 52, 129
doubling 53, 56–57, 102, 141
Douthit, Lue 4, 22, 25, 30, 32, 35, 57, 58, 59, 104, 118
Dr. Faustus (Marlowe) xiii, 12, 13, 14, 36–37, 42, 59–61, 94
Dramatists Guild of America 133–134, 144

dramaturgy 66, 97, 107–108, 109, 118, 125, 128–130, 134
drolls (performance) 20
Duchess of Malfi, The (Webster) 72–74, 78–83, 87–88, 89, 93–94

editions 36, 38–40, 47; edition v. text 38–40
Empty Space, The (Brook) 128
Evans, James 24, 35, 54, 120, 126
Every Man in His Humour (Jonson) 40, 57
Everyman (Anonymous) 83–84, 87, 88
Every Man Out of His Humour (Jonson) 100

Fellowes, Julian 60, 62
First Folio, The (Shakespeare) 13–14, 16, 19, 40–41, 42, 43–45
Folger Shakespeare (editions) 36, 37, 44, 144
Folger Shakespeare Library xiii
Freytag's Pyramid 30–31

Garrick, David xiii, 20, 124
Ghosts (Ibsen) 4, 30–31
Glass Menagerie, The (Williams) 42–43
Globe Theatre (Elizabethan playhouse) 14, 27
Green-Rogers, Martine Kei 8, 22, 25, 27, 35, 54, 94, 118

Hall, Katori 132
Hamlet (1996 film) 19
Hamlet (Q1) 14, 54
Hamlet (Shakespeare) 1, 2, 4, 11, 12, 13, 14, 16, 17, 18, 24, 30, 40, 43, 44, 46, 58, 62, 67–68, 81, 86, 88–89, 118
Hedda Gabler (Ibsen) 25, 63–65
Henry the Fourth, Part One (Shakespeare) 66
Henry the Fourth, Part Two (Shakespeare) 66
Henry the Sixth, Part One (Shakespeare) 38, 64, 75–76
Henry the Sixth, Part Two (Shakespeare) 64, 75–76
Henry the Sixth, Part Three (Shakespeare) 64, 75–76
Hinman, Charlton 46
Homelife (Albee) 137–138
Hugo, Victor-François 52
Hutcheon, Linda 52

Ibsen, Henrik 4, 24, 25, 30–31, 38, 52, 63–65, 102, 129
Importance of Being Earnest, The (Wilde) 29
intermissions 19, 31–32, 57–58

Jadhwani, Lavina 100
Jenga 5–6
Jonson, Ben 14, 18, 20, 22, 36, 38, 40, 57, 92–93, 95, 100, 108
Julius Caesar (Shakespeare) 56, 58

Kaiser, Scott 32, 102
King Lear (Shakespeare) 16, 17, 40, 53
Knight of the Burning Pestle, The (Beaumont) 40, 57
Kyd, Thomas 13, 14

Lange, Scott xiii, 34
lexicons 37–38
line bartering 125–126
line numbers 45–46
Lomma, Jonathan 132
Love for Love (Congreve) 19
Lower Depths, The (Gorky) 68–71

Macbeth (Shakespeare) 11, 16, 25, 46, 51, 52, 55, 76, 92, 107
Machinal (Treadwell) 53, 109, 110
Man and Superman (Shaw) 3, 19
Marlowe, Christopher 12, 13, 14, 42, 59–61, 95, 106
Marowitz, Charles 55, 139
Mayberry, Katherine xiii, 115, 126–127
McDonough, Megan xiii, 35, 38, 64, 121
Measure for Measure (Shakespeare) 8, 18, 92
mechanics 77–96; meter 77–85; personal rhetoric 88–92; pronouns and embedded stage directions 92–94; rhetoric 85–88; rhyme 83–85
microcasts 101–102
Midsummer Night's Dream, A (Shakespeare) xiii, 22, 54, 58, 62, 95, 99, 106, 124, 126, 127
Miss Julie (Strindberg) xiii, 29, 63
Modenessi, Alfredo Michel 59
Molière 110, 135
Morris, Cass xiii, 86–87
Much Ado About Nothing (1993 film) 23
Much Ado About Nothing (Shakespeare) 2, 23, 110, 119

Mudge, Grant 23, 99
Mulvany, Kate 2, 35, 56, 71, 101, 107, 111–112, 118

Northam, Anna 106

Oedipus Rex (Sophocles) 25, 31, 62
Oregon Shakespeare Festival, The 4, 22, 35, 54, 102, 104
Oswald, Peter 12, 138–139
Othello (Shakespeare) xiii, 40, 95

Packer, Tina 7, 32, 35, 55–56, 116, 119
parallel-text analysis xiii, 16–17, 38–39, 123
performance editions 11, 13–14, 40, 41, 44, 125
Pigeon Creek Shakespeare Company (Grand Rapids, MI) xiii, 114–115
Poorboy Theatre (Scotland) xiii
presentation 46–47, 119–123
public domain 7, 41, 57, 69, 127, 128, 131–135, 137
Public Theater's Shakespeare in Central Park (NY) 35
Public Works (NY) 108

quartos 13–14, 15, 16, 40–41, 42, 43–45
Queen Margaret (McDonough) xiii, 64

reasons for cutting 16–20; time 16; politics 16; audiences 17; dumb jokes 17; clarity 18
Richard III (Shakespeare) xiii, 2, 8, 20, 64, 98, 103, 111–116, 126–127
ROADS to Rhetoric 86–88; repetition 86; omission 86; addition 86–87; direction 87; substitution 88
Roberts-Smith, Jennifer xiii, 111
Romeo and Juliet (2013 film) 60, 62
Romeo and Juliet (Shakespeare) 15, 25, 40, 43, 48–49, 50–51, 54, 58, 71–72, 87, 89–90, 129
Romeo Y Julieta (Modenessi) 59
Royal National Theatre (London), The 97, 98, 108
Royal Shakespeare Company, The 108, 109, 125
run time, calculating 32–34

Schmidle, Christine 13, 15, 17, 31, 75–76
Seagull, The (Chekhov) 55, 101

Second Shepherd's Play, The (The Wakefield Master) 84–85, 86
Shakespeare & Company (Lenox, MA) 7, 32
Shakespeare, William xiii, 1, 2, 4, 10, 11, 12, 13, 14, 15, 16, 17–18, 20, 22, 24, 25, 30, 31, 32, 34, 38, 40, 43, 46, 48–49, 50–51, 52, 53, 54, 55, 56, 58, 59, 62, 64, 66, 67–68, 71–72, 74–75, 75–76, 81, 86, 88–89, 89–90, 92, 95, 98, 99, 106, 107, 108, 109, 110, 111–116, 118, 119, 124, 125, 126–127, 129, 135
Shakespeare's Globe (London reproduction) 31
Shapiro, James xiii, 3, 11, 35, 36, 37, 59, 98, 102, 108, 125
Sharing Your Cut 38, 119–125
Shaw, George Bernard 1, 3, 5, 19, 20, 24, 94
Shaw Festival (Canada), The 19
SITI Company (NY), The 127
Sophocles 24, 25, 31, 36, 38, 62
Stratford Festival (Canada), The 18, 35, 55, 58, 104, 105, 108
Synetic Theater (Virginia) 52

talkbacks 119, 129–130
Tempest, The (Shakespeare) 20, 108, 109
Three Questions, The 22–34, 102, 109, 140; 1: Who is My Audience? 23–28; 2: What is My Story? 28–31; 3: How Much Time do I have? 31–34
Through Line Numbering (TLN) 46
To the Mountaintop (Hall) 132
touring 10, 12, 14, 17, 18–19, 23, 25, 57, 97, 98, 99, 102, 106–107, 126, 133
Twelfth Night (Shakespeare) 18, 31, 74–75, 108

University of Waterloo (Canada) xiii, 113

venue 14, 16, 97, 99, 103–106, 107, 115
virtual logistics 99, 108–111
visualization 30–31, 38, 59–61
Volpone (Jonson) 15, 22, 92–93

Waiting for Godot (Beckett) 131, 137
Webster, John 20, 72–74, 78–83, 87–88, 89, 93–94, 95
Who's Afraid of Virginia Woolf? (Albee) 132, 138
Wilde, Oscar 24, 29, 36

word clouds xiii, 59–61
word replacement 58–60

Yirra Yaakin Theatre Company (Perth, Australia) 107–108

Young, TJ 136
YouTube 97, 108, 136

Zoo Story, The (Albee) 137–138
ZOOM (videoconferencing) 108–109

For Product Safety Concerns and Information please contact our EU
representative GPSR@taylorandfrancis.com
Taylor & Francis Verlag GmbH, Kaufingerstraße 24, 80331 München, Germany

www.ingramcontent.com/pod-product-compliance
Lightning Source LLC
Chambersburg PA
CBHW061350300426
44116CB00011B/2065